Endorsements

"One of the greatest gifts of love we can offer another is to journey with them as they are dying. The capacity to do this is not restricted to a selected few, nor should it be, for the time will come when we want to be that companion or we will be asked to be the friend, midwife, or amicus for one who is dying. In this small, beautifully written and stirring handbook, Deanna Cochran tells us how we can be advocates for those who are dying, preserve their precious normality, and be part of a loving, caring team. For some, this book will prepare you for the occasion when you need to care for a dying loved one. For others, it may be the incentive to take this gift of caring into the wider community. It is a book for the times—a book that empowers individuals and gives them the courage to confront and overcome their fears and doubts about caring for another."
  ~ **Dr. Michael Barbato,** Author of *Midwifing Death*

"In the United States alone, 10,000 people will turn 65 years old every day for the next 18 years. In the same ways these baby boomers live their lives, the awareness and priority they place on quality of life continues to grow as well. This applies to how they live and age, as well as how they face the end-of-life and grieve the loss of their loved ones. Deanna Cochran leverages her years of multifaceted training and broad experience in healthcare, empowering those interested in becoming world class in serving the dying through doula-type services. These educational and occupational services Deanna provides are timely, opportune, and tightly aligned with the mentality, philosophies, and priorities of the boomer demographic."
  ~ **Jay A. Drayer, CPA**, Founder/CEO of
  CareFlash (for people) and PrizedPals (for pet families)

"Deanna Cochran's book overflows with experiential wisdom one can acquire only through years of nursing, hospice care, accompanying the dying, deep listening, honest assessments of 'the death trade,' human fears surrounding death, and well-honed personal instincts. As an end-of-life midwife and trainer, Deanna brings a wealth of accumulated knowledge to her ministry and now shares her excellent insights for everyone to explore and take to heart in the chapters of this profound book. Read it and learn. You will be enlightened!"

~ Rev. Jo Jensen, DMin, BCC, Author of
The Be-Attitudes of Chaplaincy

"I remember in the 1970s being interested in the end-of-life (a term not actually used until recently) and wondering how I could best be of service. Oh, if only I'd had a book like this one. The guidance, honesty, and direction would have been just what I needed.

"There have been a lot of changes in end-of-life care since the 1970s—hospice and palliative care are now household terms. With this exposure comes an awakening in the hearts of servers, those people who hear the call to work with end-of-life. Deanna, with *Accompanying the Dying: A Practical Guide and Awareness Training*, has provided the tolls to find the way. This book presents a great deal of information in an easily flowing manner, and with just enough personal stories to warm the education."

~ Barbara Karnes, RN, Author of
Gone from My Sight

"A comprehensive introduction to working as an end-of-life doula. Deanna's longtime experience as a hospice nurse and her deep and heartfelt commitment to education are evident on every page. If you're called to care for people in the last stages of life, this book will help you begin the journey."

~ Sarah Kerr, PhD
Death Doula and Celebrant

"Being with an individual who is dying or taking their final breath of life is the greatest gift you can give an individual and they can give you. Learn to be consciously present with the dying through Deanna's heartfelt teachings. In 1986, when I started working with the dying, I wish I'd had her book, *Accompanying the Dying*."

~ **Rev. Sharon Lund, DD,** Author of
Sacred Living, Sacred Dying: A Guide to Embracing Life and Death

"As we reclaim death, dying, and ceremony back into our own hands, and hold it in its natural and sacred place within our lives, Deanna offers her vast experience, enthusiasm, and wisdom to assist others to travel this journey well. Her generosity of spirit and her ability to share her knowledge and insights through this book allow people to have a friend to support them in planning ahead or in a challenging time."

~ **Zenith Virago**, Deathwalker
Coauthor of *The Intimacy of Dying and Death*

"For anyone heeding the call of an end-of-life vocation in any form or expression, Deanna Cochran's voice rings clear. The work she inspires spans the great divide between service and quest, joining the practical to the compassionate, encompassing self-care and patient care in ways that prepare anyone from any background or goal to participate and grow. This is Deanna's superpower: encouraging and enriching personal, emotional, and spiritual growth around death to free those committed to offering death care services to be fully present and effective. By coming prepared and grounded, end-of-life advocates—including home funeral guides—are truly ready to take up the challenges and joys of supporting families through the death of a loved one."

~ **Lee Webster**, President
National Home Funeral Alliance

"Like an artisan creating a fine tapestry, Deanna Cochran, in her book *Accompanying the Dying*, weaves together varicolored threads from her experience as a hospice nurse, a death doula, a spiritual seeker, a teacher, and a caregiver for her dying mother. She has filled these pages with inspiring stories, practical knowledge, and wise guidance for living and dying consciously. This book is a must-read for anyone who feels called to sit at the bedside of the dying, whether caring for a loved one or starting a new career path as an end-of-life worker. Deanna Cochrane is the teacher you need for your journey into the mysteries of life and death."

~ **Dr. Karen Wyatt**, Author of
The Tao of Death

"Deanna brings a truly wise voice to this social movement about reclaiming community-centered death care. Her words speak sincerely to those who feel called to serve the dying, dead, and bereaved. Regardless of what titles we volunteers and practitioners use to refer to ourselves, Deanna's writing describes the shared passion, compassion, and competencies that ground us in this precious and culturally relevant work."

~ **Cassandra Yonder**, Executive Director of
BEyond Yonder Virtual School
for Community Deathcaring in Canada

Accompanying the Dying

Accompanying the Dying

Practical, Heart-Centered Wisdom
for End-of-Life Doulas and Healthcare Advocates

Deanna Cochran, RN
EOL Doula, Mentor and Trainer
Founder of Quality of Life Care, LLC

Contents

This book is dedicated to my mother, Patricia Doyle Flores. She envisioned me teaching and holding workshops when I was running all over central Austin as a hospice nurse with no awareness or desire to do such a thing. Her dying and death have inspired my work as an end-of-life doula and advocate since 2005.

This book is also dedicated to my father. To me, he is such an inspiration in living your dreams and taking action on what you love to do. As we journey with him through end-stage cardiac disease, he has been my greatest teacher about living life to the fullest.

I especially honor all the people who let me into their world to accompany them and their families as they lived and died. Without you, I would not have been able to care for my mother the way I did. Without you, I'd have nothing to share.

And last but not least, this book is dedicated to all the courageous men and women who have trusted me and allowed me into their dreams of serving others at the end of life and asking me to help them take inspired action. I'm proud of your faith and bravery to trailblaze in this unfamiliar territory of dying well in the modern age. I'm honored to walk beside you as you empower your communities. Together, we are making great strides in this grassroots movement. I love you and thank you for bringing me into your world.

Foreword

I will tell you right up front that I have some ambivalence about the new group of specialists having names like "death doulas" and "death midwives" and many other names Deanna has heard. "Death sitter" was one I came up with. I knew "minister of death" wouldn't fly.

I'm ambivalent because one of the many hats I sometimes wear is called "death doula," and I also offer training for death doulas. At the same time, one of the threads of the tapestry I am weaving is the reclaiming by families and communities of the care of the dying and the dead.

We gave this work away to what have become big businesses and institutions. Having given it away, we robbed ourselves of deep, powerful, and important work that awakens us to life, builds communities, connects families, and guides us on the path of grieving. After all, at the core of a community are the ways we care for each other.

I am concerned that death doula will become another career path, a profession of so-called experts, regulated by new agencies that wish to legitimize and standardize, and will itself become its own institution defined and confined by what it is and isn't.

It's very tricky, as it turns out, naming something.

Dying at this time, in this culture, has become predominantly a medical and psychological event.

Clearly, dying is so much more. That there is "so much more" is rarely acknowledged or given the attention it requires. Many of us see an important and essential gap that needs to be addressed.

How did this gap come about, and what are some of the effects?

> ➢ We are so disconnected from the natural world and our place in it. We don't see that there is no life without death and that death feeds life. We

of the modern era have lost our way. We have forgotten who we are, why we are here, and what it means to be truly human. To a large degree, we are sleepwalking through life, leaning forward into what's next. Our materialistic view discounts much of what cannot be qualified and quantified and magnifies our tremendous fear of being dead.

➤ The undercurrent of death as a mistake, a failure, or a punishment still resounds loudly in the conscious and unconscious collective.

➤ *Dead* and *death* have almost become taboo words in our culture. The tree dies; the car dies; the dog dies. Grandma hardly ever dies. She passes, passes away, transitions, leaves her body, graduates, and so on. She's gone to a better place (hopefully); we've lost Grandma; she's gone home. All these euphemisms have tremendous implications.

➤ Death, having moved from the home and village life to the hospital and the funeral home, is rarely, if ever, experienced by most of us. We, in general, have little or no direct experience with people actively dying or with their death or with the dead. This often leaves the dying and their family clueless, terrified, and feeling incompetent.

➤ The many subtle and not-so-subtle ways our cultural and personal avoidance of, aversion to, and denial of death show up in how we live, how we view dying and death, and how we treat the dying and the dead.

➤ Few in this culture see any value in the process of actively dying, and most people wish for the dying process to happen as quickly as possible. Near-death experiences are on the best-seller list, but these are different from the near-death experience of finding out you're dying, and the terror and shock often accompanying the news.

At the very least, a death doula, having likely been around dying and death a whole lot more than the dying person and his or her family, can be a reassuring presence and a witness to the process.

Death happens! We show up for death. In fact, this may be a death doula's most important function.

Yes, there are herbs, potions, and medicines. Yes, there are visualizations and practices for approaching the doorway. Yes, there are skill sets for supporting a dying person to do the work of completing his or her life and to approach death facing forward, as well as supporting the work family members are engaged in. Yes, there are numerous maps for what happens after death.

But almost anyone can learn all this. What cannot be learned is what it takes to fully show up for dying and death and not turn away, as so many dying people seem to do these days or, for that matter, what it takes to show up fully to life, since few people seem to.

Yes, the groundwork can begin. There is much to do to uncover our own conscious and unconscious beliefs and stories that get in the way—owning and disowning our own fears, projections, and judgments.

Still, when we give something a name, create a role, and define the role, we box it in and reduce it.

In a culture where one of the first questions we ask, and are asked, is, "And what do you do," after we tell them, the next question will likely be, "And what is a death doula?" or "What does a death doula do?" And we nail the box further.

The paradox here is that those I run across who are called to this work do not see themselves working in the already-boxed-in roles of chaplain, social worker, hospice nurse, or grief counselor.

Now here comes this book by Deanna Cochran, whom I met some years back when she came to see what I was up to and who this guy was who opened a store named The Death Store. I was immediately taken in by her eyes and her smile and by how easily her heart expressed through her words, and I could see how her work was defined in relation to her heart. We became instant friends and have proceeded to learn from each other.

To me, she's the perfect person to write about this subject. Deanna has had many years of experience in working at the bedsides of the dying, in being with their families, and in teaching and counseling other professionals in these fields. And in her very down-to-earth way, she brings this emerging field to the layperson and to those already working as healers and counselors.

Deanna has dedicated many years to looking deeply into what end-of-life care is asking of all of us when we are dying and when we are caring for the dying. You may be feeling a call to this work, or what I refer to as *sacred service*. It matters little what it is called; it becomes ministry. And as such, our work is framed by listening and following the call. We learn to listen deeply on the inside, and we also learn to listen deeply at the bedside of the dying.

~ Rev. Bodhi Be
Founder, Doorway Into Light

Introduction

Do You Engage with Dying and Death, or Do You Run from It?

Accompanying the dying is not something most people dream about wanting to do. So, if you are one of us who share a deep desire to do so, know this: You are not weird or morbid. Consider yourself a light bearer, a healer of anxiety, a soother, and a stabilizing force for people during one of the most frightening and grievous periods of their lives.

I knew I wanted to serve privately, one family at a time, after the death of my mother, in the summer of 2005. She went into the hospital via EMS on Mother's Day 2005 and was dead the Wednesday before Father's Day.

My mother did not want hospice. She wanted to live, and she wanted to try alternative treatments. She also wanted the surgery the oncologist had recommended. She wanted to go to Brazil and see John of God. We were getting our white outfits together to do that with her. We developed our own palliative care team, which consisted of me, (a hospice nurse), a hospice nurse friend in Austin (our doula), my sister (a nurse anesthetist) and her friends in the medical field, and an oncologist who begrudgingly gave us morphine (for her pain) and a hospice referral just ten days before she died. (He was convinced that he could do surgery on her in the upcoming months.)

On that last office visit, 10 days before her death, we walked into his office, with my mother literally half-dead (she would not cancel the appointment). She could barely walk. I had to guide her everywhere we went to as she had seemed to forget where she was going. I had to hold her up and prop her up and found a place for her to lie as she could not sit up for long. When we finally were in the doctor's office, I nearly came unglued when he suggested surgery, refused to prescribe stronger pain medication for her increasing pain, and would not give us a hospice referral. I knew that my mother would be unhappy if I were to have a full-out temper tantrum in his office, and that was more important than my urge to fly across his desk with rage.

When we left his office and had made it to the car, she looked at me and smiled. She asked me, "Am I dying?" She had asked me to be honest with her. I told her, "Yes." She asked how much time she had. I told her my best guess was under a month. She smiled and said that poor man (the doctor) didn't know how to handle telling her. I explained that she was getting to the point where she really needed the kind of care that only hospice can give, that I could not provide the perspective anymore to help deal with her symptoms, which could get more complicated quickly. I told her that she had been receiving palliative care all along anyway; let's just please bring more support. She finally agreed. She died ten days later.

Over the years, I have come to understand that some oncologists do not know what dying and imminent death look like (as we expect them to), or surely they would never say the kinds of things the physician said to us that day (with my mother staring straight through him, as people do right before they lose consciousness during the dying process).

Despite not having an "official palliative care team" my mother didn't spend a single day in the hospital due to any symptoms of this very aggressive cancer because she had excellent palliative care from the professionals in our circle. I knew that the protocols that hospice used were appropriate for people not on hospice services. We made it possible for her to have what she needed. There were few palliative care programs (non-hospice) in 2005, and at the time, I had no idea there was such a thing as palliative care prior to hospice. It was virtually unheard of, even in hospice circles, even now (in 2018).

Sometime in the days following her death, I knew that I wanted everyone going through dying to have "a hospice nurse for a daughter" when he or she was going through dying because so many people are not dying on hospice service. Like most people's, my mother's dying mostly occurred off hospice service. Again, like most people, only her imminent dying period occurred on hospice.

Over the years, it has seemed to me that many people avoid the topic of death and tend to keep their distance when it is happening in their social circles. What has been your experience? Those of us who want to accompany others actually find joy in serving at this time. We *want* to be there. A powerful inner energy fuels us to look for ways to help others at this time. It is the same joy you hear expressed when at other times people are deeply in service to one another.

We who are called are advocates for the dying and their families. We are people who want to bring light to a topic cloaked in fear and dread. People will often say they want to bring peace and beauty to this final sacred transition from this earthly plane, where there is presently chaos and avoidance. We want to bring it out of the shadows. We want to bring normalcy to dying and accompanying the dying, to be something that everyone feels comfortable doing, not just people like us.

For the past several years in my end-of-life doula mentoring program, students have reported that they are, or have been, the "go-to" person within the circle of family and friends when someone is ill or dying. (Sometimes this has not been the case. I have worked with people who have never seen someone die but knew deep inside they wanted to be of service in this way.)

So who are we? Who are the souls who want to accompany others through their final days? Are we strange or death-obsessed? Do we find joy in others' misery? What are our motives? Why are we investing so much of our time, energy, and money so we can help complete strangers as they die? Why don't we just work for hospice instead of creating a private practice? Why are chaplains, social workers, physicians, and nurses exploring their desire to serve on this more intimate path?

We are all sorts of people, in all kinds of professions, and most of us do it for the same reason: we are *called*. The minute we received that calling from a higher spiritual plane, we *knew* this was what we wanted to do. Many people I have spoken to over the years have shared with me they had been thinking about serving the dying for many years before they began.

Outside of hospice professionals, who use the roles of hospice to serve, most other people called will remain the knowledgeable go-to person in their circle. Of those, only a few will continue onward to serve their community. I talk with people every day about their beginnings, and I usually discover that it was a personal experience with the dying of someone they cared about that drew them to want to serve more people or to serve on a deeper level.

So, I write this book because in the years since I made the decision to serve as an end-of life doula, thousands of people have contacted me wanting to do the same thing. In 2010, I created my process to help others to accompany patients who matched their skill set and their desire to serve their circle of family and friends or their communities. To be sure, this is something anyone can do for their family and friends. It is the people who have the passion to do it for strangers in the community and change the way we die in this society whom I focus mostly upon in this book.

In 2012, I began to receive inquiries from professionals within mainstream healthcare who wanted to deepen their practice of serving the dying or add it to the services they already provided. It has been a very rewarding time indeed. The only thing I enjoy more than mentoring other doulas is personally serving a family. I feel very blessed and grateful that I followed my heart and kept doing the next right thing, which led me to write this for you.

True, those of us who are medical can offer other services, but that is not what makes us a great doula. What makes a great doula is a compassionate presence, a loving heart, attentiveness, and a fearlessness toward dying or death, whether our own or someone else's.

Presence does not require a college degree, medical credentials, a high school diploma, a thesis, and years of experience. It takes a spiritual practice, self-care, self-awareness, a connection to life and humanity, and nourishment of the soul, however you do that; no one religion or spiritual practice corners the market on these items. How do you maintain this quality? What do you do to have this peaceful quality of presence?

The book is divided into five parts to address the different realms of the work of end-of-life advocacy.

Please note: For simplicity, I will use the term *end-of-life doula* when referring to the go-to person within a family and any person, regardless of what he or she calls himself or herself (death doula, end-of-life practitioner, death midwife, soul midwife, doula for the dying, end-of-life coach, etc.), who serves others through dying. I refer to this role as End-of Life Doula because there has been traction for that title over the last years, and it is actually what is "sticking" within mainstream healthcare who utilize the role. And mainstream healthcare is where most of the people are that we wish to empower. We want to be a useful, powerful adjunct for the health care systems that presently care for our dying. Our role has that ability—to serve families as well as the systems who serve families.

Also, for the most part, I do not include URLs (internet addresses) for organizations and articles because they change so often. You can put these titles of articles or organizations in a Google, Yahoo, or Bing search bar and find them for more information.

For the person who feels inspired to dive more deeply into this material with Deanna, know that you are welcome in our school of Accompanying the Dying. It is a human skill not just for professionals. Learn more here:
www.school.accompanyingthedying.com.

PART I

Where We Are Now

In this section, I explore the awakening that is occurring around the world. There are many beautiful, generous, and wise souls who want to step forth and serve others in unique ways. They are light bearers in what can be some people's darkest hours. They want to spread empowerment to people in their communities about options and choices. They want to be part of dispelling fear and anxiety about dying and death. This "death positive" movement is growing and changing rapidly for those of us who are knee-deep in this work. Those of us who have been around a while (longer than the last five or six years) have seen an explosive growth. Yet we are still invisible to the majority of the population. We will be here, though, when people wake up and want to learn for themselves or need our assistance.

Chapter 1

Who Are the Death Workers Now?

We're all just walking each other home.
~ Ram Dass

In 2018, when we think of people who work with the dying, we may think of hospice employees and hospice volunteers, as well as people who work in hospitals and such frontline responders as emergency workers, paramedics, and firefighters. We know people die in hospitals and nursing homes on a regular basis. We know that people who work in these settings are seeing a lot of dying and participate in trying to prevent death. Unless hospice is involved, most people employed in these settings are trying to keep you alive.

There is also an emerging trend whereby people drawn to serve, as independent practitioners are becoming part of the "death positive movement" or "death empowerment movement." These people are called many things, but they are basically offering particular services: accompanying people as they are imminently dying, providing guidance for home funerals and home burials, and providing such interesting bereavement services as bedside singing, celebrant services, and living wakes.

Some people are creating concierge services at the end of life, patient advocacy services, and assistance with advance directives. A lot is going on within this realm of life because, until now, we had been satisfied with trying to live at all costs, and we were paying for that with personal and family chaos and indignity. As a society, we are done with this.

Chapter 2

Why Don't We Just Work for Hospice?

Whenever you go, go with all your heart.
~ Confucius

So many people doing this work *are* working for hospice. Many of us are volunteers, as well. We love it and feel useful there. Something else is also happening.

Many want to serve in in more unique, non-medical ways and spend more time with people than we now can within hospice because, within hospice, we must work within our role, and our role is clearly defined. Some people want to help in a different way than what hospice allows. And most every person who calls me says they want to be able to spend more time with the people they serve.

First, to channel this desire to work with the dying, if you work within hospice as an employee, you must be one of a certain occupation: certified nursing assistant, nurse, social worker, chaplain, physician, or nurse practitioner. You could also volunteer in your free time.

As a society, we have come to love and depend on each of these professionals as experts in the care of the dying. These roles are clearly defined and have limits. They need to for organizations that provide hospice services serve millions of people and need to have a specific structure within which to operate. Hospice is an amazing system on which we have come to depend, and, they too are seeking innovative ways to continue to deepen their support at the end of life.

Each role on the hospice team is also limited by the amount of time they can spend with a family and by the organization's policies and procedures. A volunteer is limited by what the organization has openings for and by how the hospice wants the volunteer to serve and some hospices have strict time limits. The family is limited by the availability of volunteers and by whether one will serve the family as it desires. So, although for many volunteers and families, this system works wonderfully, and people's needs are met just fine, there is plenty of room for adjunctive support that provides more time. No one agency exists at this time that can take the place of hospice. However, we are seeing that with the changing of the Medicare benefit in the United States even when someone is on hospice services, at times more support is needed.

Every hospice nurse who has written me has been intrigued by this role and wants to know more about this phenomenon of the end-of-life doula/guide/midwife. Recently, someone misunderstood our purpose and thought we were trying to take the place of hospice. She also thought we wanted to do tasks and services for which we were not qualified. Please hear me on this: there is no replacing hospice—*ever*. Hospice services have their place, thank goodness. We end-of-life doulas are support people *in addition to* hospice. Here was my reply to her concern:

> *I have been a hospice nurse for 18 years, and in my experience as a hospice nurse and as a private [end-of-life] doula, I know there is much to be improved in end-of-life support. Everyone knows that and is trying their best to do it. (Some notable physicians who are advocating for better end-of-life care are Dr. Atwal Gwande, Dr. Ira Byock, Dr. Jessica Zitter, Dr. Timothy Ihrig . . . among many others.)*
>
> *Palliative care has come a long way, and leaders in the field continue to support improvement. Hospice, when it first came out, was outside of the medical system and was brought within it. I understand where you are coming from. I, too, have had my loved ones die with hospice and was blessed by the experience.*
>
> *I think you may have misunderstood the role of doulas. They are an adjunct to any team caring for someone. They are not planning the care. Just like any caregiver, they are welcomed and skilled (up to their level of expertise) and have a calling to serve, just like you and me. They are in no way trying to take the place of hospice—ever. I suggest strongly to every person I work with to volunteer with hospice. I train hospice volunteers as well. We all know our place. Please understand that no one I work with would ever misconstrue his or her place.*
>
> *And as regards to payment for services, we are hired by families and yes, most doulas I know, myself included, provide their services for free to those in need. Many people can easily afford caregivers and our services, yet others*

cannot. All doulas I know serve whoever crosses their path the best way they can. So many beautiful souls want to help and serve the dying and yet are not called to be a nurse, chaplain, social worker, or CNA or physician; still, they are serving in amazing ways.

I'd love to talk to you and share with you more about doulas so you understand that we in no way are replacing anything that is happening now. We are adding to the support, and people love it. Hospices love it when I'm around, as I help them and add to the secure feeling all around. If you'd like to talk further, feel free to call me.

~Deanna Cochran

Chapter 3

The Death Trade

*You will not be good teachers if you focus only on
what you do and not upon who you are.
~ Rudolf Steiner*

Stephen Jenkinson, notable leader in transforming the way we think about death in the world, calls the business of caring for the dying (outside of family members) *the death trade*. *The death trade* has a chilling feel to it. Yet all who serve the dying, outside of volunteers, are being paid to do so. Greed soils everything, not money. Money is the currency that enables us all to pay our bills, plan for our old age, and travel or otherwise enjoy life.

Energy and/or money is being exchanged on every level to care for our dying. We have medical professionals through hospice, hospitals, and home health companies. And we have practical and caregiving assistance through private services, which people pay for out of pocket. All of this is valuable help. The people caring for us in all these scenarios must pay their bills; we want them to. Why would anyone be upset about that? It does not take the sacred away from the service to be paid for your time and energy. We sometimes encounter some shameful and angry energy around being paid for spiritual services and death care, so let's talk about the evolution of death care for a moment.

Prior to the time when hospitals and funeral directors handled everything people died young and at home and were buried in the family plot or cemeteries by family and friends. We romanticize this period in the present end-of-life movement as a time of control and of meaningful personal and community involvement in the dying, death, and after-death care of our loved ones. People knew death intimately, saw it often, and saw many young people dying. People died from disease pretty swiftly and from accidents and war. Many women died in childbirth; many children died before their first birthday. I have been told by more than one elderly storyteller that they did not like dealing with death back then any more than we do now. They were just as grief-stricken and tried to avoid it perhaps, but they could not.

So today, people are dying much differently. People are surviving childhood, living decades longer (albeit in more unhealthy conditions), and dying much more slowly from chronic diseases. We are using technology to prolong our inevitable death and are having great difficulty as a society deciding what we feel is moral regarding allowing people to die naturally without these amazing interventions. We can keep people alive now despite all odds, and we ask ourselves, "Yes, but should we?" We are realizing that the hospital may not be a great place to be when you are dying, and more people are realizing this and wanting to die at home.

In the early 1900s, people did die at home, mostly with their families. During this time, hospitals were being seen as a place to go for the possibility of cure. Before then, hospitals were a place that took care of the poor, an extension of charitable institutions known as "almshouses," and they didn't have much money. Most physicians donated their time.

Advances in cleanliness, surgery, and medicine swept the world in the ensuing decades. Hospitals wanted to appeal to the affluent. They became affiliated with educational institutions. At the same time, the funeral industry was positioning itself as a replacement for the family "parlor." Embalming became the norm; at death, people were being transported to a professional setting to prepare the body for burial in local cemeteries, and US cemeteries were created for veterans instead of burying veterans on family land.

Little did we know that we were setting ourselves up for the suffering we now experience. We have progressed beyond the marvels of medicine to the horrors of dying in present-day America in our intensive care units. Nurses and physicians tell me all the time how unsettling it is in our best hospitals to be doing what they do to people who are dying. We are all responsible. We are all responsible for how we got into this mess, and we are all responsible for getting ourselves out of it.

When treatment is used at appropriate times, added quality of life is exactly the result; but when treatment is used on a dying person, misery happens instead. For the last twenty-five years or so, physician authors Atwul Gawande, Michael Barbato, Ira Byock, and Timothy Ihrig have been telling us about this.

Along with the professionals in the death trade, entering our landscape are many wise souls, with no nurse or doctor or chaplain or social worker credential who want to help us die well. Within mainstream healthcare and without, we are responding to the call that we can do better than this as we die. We are in a grassroots movement right now empowering each other to die well. Can you sense it and see it around you that people want to know more about dying well? Do you notice that more and more people are 'talking about death? These are the first necessary steps to begin transforming our naïve way of looking at dying and death in our modern world.

More of us are realizing that *we* are responsible for having a peaceful dying experience. *We* must let everyone know what we want, make sure that it's written somewhere, and have someone close to us who can access those documents and speak on our behalf, should we be unable to do so. Our default is saving your life at all costs. If you want to be allowed to die naturally, you must plan for it and have it in writing. We are beginning to have these conversations.

Chapter 4

What Could Possibly Be Beyond Hospice?

The measure of intelligence is the ability to change.
~ Albert Einstein

Before June 15, 2005 (the day my mother died), I never thought of serving people privately. I was on hiatus as a hospice nurse for a long-term acute-care facility, taking a break from all the dying of the previous five years. It is interesting that during this "break," my focus in the hospital was on who was dying and on how to help them get to the hospice house for proper support or get them home and in the comfort of their family and friends with hospice. I was a fierce advocate for the dying there, and I'm sure I drove everyone nuts. I can't tell you how many times a physician told me, "Deanna, you always think everyone is dying," or "Deanna, he just has a cold, for crying out loud!" or "Give him another breathing treatment and everything will be all right," and then would laugh at me and shake his or her head. I don't blame them; they just didn't know that they were staring death straight in the eye. They didn't have the experience with it that I had had during the prior five years. They didn't have the training in palliative care.

Palliative care and the knowledge of palliative care applied prior to hospice services is one area that is beyond hospice. (See "Palliative Care" in the Supplemental Materials section.) Hospice deals only with the terminally ill, whereas palliative care is for *all* diagnoses and should begin from day 1 of a diagnosis. A lot of dying is happening outside of hospice. Many people suffer for years with advanced, end-stage illness prior to their death, and palliative medicine is *the* medicine for this group. Thus, a doula needs to know palliative care well.

> What *is* palliative care? According to *Get Palliative Care*:
> *Palliative Care* (pronounced *pal*-lee-uh-tiv) *is specialized medical care for people with serious illness. It focuses on providing relief from the symptoms and stress of a serious illness. The goal is to improve quality of life for both the patient and the family.*
>
> *Palliative care is provided by a specially trained team of doctors, nurses, social workers and other specialists who work together with a patient's doctors to provide an extra layer of support. It is appropriate at any age and at any stage in a serious illness and can be provided along with curative treatment.*

More and more hospitals, home-health agencies, and clinics are including the specialty of palliative medicine, utilizing it long before hospice is even appropriate or considered.

Another area where end-of-life doulas can make a huge difference is in the time of pre-death vigil. Hospice is not a caregiving agency; it is more of a consulting agency with specialty services. Professionals such as nurses, chaplains, social workers, certified nursing assistants (CNAs), nurse practitioners, and sometimes physicians will come to where the person is dying (in home, hospital, or nursing home), assess his or her status, and initiate interventions that will be helpful physically, emotionally, and spiritually for the person who is dying and his or her whole family. But hospice is not set up to help care for your loved one.

Hospice has volunteer services and another benefit called *continuous care* that may be helpful during the days preceding death, but the availability of volunteers will determine whether you get one, and strict criteria must be met for continuous care. Sometimes families feel they need much more support, which mostly translates to more time spend with them, during these days than hospice can provide. End–of-life doulas are invaluable here. Furthermore, at death, most hospices stop the services of the care team that was visiting the family prior to death and put the family in contact with a bereavement coordinator instead. It is a different team member, new to the family. The transfer of care can be unsettling to a family. The seamless service of a doula between the pre- and post-death of a family member is very soothing for the family.

Another area where doulas can be invaluable is in how much time they can spend with a family. Unless a person qualifies for continuous care, most visits from hospice staff last an hour or less. End-of-life doula services are arranged by what the family desires, not by an agency schedule. So the hospice can utilize doula services to step in and provide loving care when a family wants or needs extra support. This level of care is normally beyond the hospice staff's ability.

Thus, there are many reasons why the service of an end-of-life doula would be wonderful. Hospice *is* invaluable, but the amount of time hospice can spend is only so much.

There are some people who are creating a practice much like a personal companion service, only with an expertise in the end of life. This type of doula is a perfect complement to hospice services. Hospices would be wise to employ doulas for their most challenging situations.

End-of-life doulas come from a variety of backgrounds, so their expertise varies. They are coming forward in droves to seek out people like me for guidance and training. Its a grassroots movement of individuals seeking to serve others at a time when almost everyone else is trying to avoid it. Some just want to be better at serving their family and friends. Some want to do more in the community. Some want to volunteer, and some want to do it for a living, not just in their after-work hours. These people want to be part of bridging the gaps in healthcare and death care. They want to serve beyond hospice.

Chapter 5

"I Thought I Made It Up"

Your heart is free, have the courage to follow it.
~ Watson, in Braveheart

So many people tell me their stories of how they thought they invented this role. They love telling of their "Aha!" moment of connecting how they could bring this desire into the world to serve the dying, "just like a birth midwife or doula." People tell me about their experiences serving their family and friends and how they realized one day that they wanted to do this for others. I hear their stories all the time.

The truth is that this is a role many of us filled just as a matter of course, "called" or not, in the carrying out of our human duties of caring for our loved ones at home as they were ill and dying.

I remember when I thought I had created this "death midwife" concept. My experience with my second daughter's birth at home with a lay midwife in 1990 was easy to translate into the end-of-life role that I wanted to take on.

I had had a high-tech C-section birth with my first child due to the decisions the physician made at the time. He did everything I asked him not to do. I did not want another experience like that. The physician who attended my first child's birth created high drama because he stepped into natural processes with his completely unnecessary interventions. He turned a normal, low-risk birthing experience into a medical intervention nightmare of the highest degree.

Because of my choice to take control of my second pregnancy and birth and not repeat that very serious life-threatening situation, I discovered that my best option at the

17

to have a home birth with midwives. I had interviewed several physicians who ...d I would be a "high-risk" pregnancy because of the previous C-section. But I felt I ...d no choice but to have my baby at home. We lived 10 minutes away from the hospital, so I felt safe that if something were "to happen," we would be close enough. After all, after my first experience, I didn't have much faith. I had supposedly been in a "safe place," the hospital, and the physician had created a very unsafe situation for my child and me.

For my second pregnancy, I was overseen by an MD who was delightful, who empowered me, and who gave me the okay, saying that I was perfectly able to have a baby "normally." Thanks, Doc, for the validation. I really needed it because that first physician actually put in my health record that I was a poor candidate for a VBAC (vaginal birth after C-section).

The healing experience of the midwives during my pregnancy, the wonderful physician who was part of my plan, and the empowerment I felt in taking charge of my health and that of my baby dramatically and significantly changed me. I knew from that time onward that, most assuredly, it was up to me to lead my healthcare, to make my wishes known, and to make things happen. If I didn't, I was going to be at the mercy of my practitioner's prevailing thoughts. *Even when I did create my birth plan with my physician, my wishes were not honored.* But, I know I did everything possible before, during and afterwards to create a safe environment and one that was meaningful to me. That is what we are called to do, take responsibility for ourselves.

So when I knew I wanted to help others feel empowered to die as they wished, it was natural for me to say, "I am a death midwife," just like those beautiful souls who gave me back my confidence at a terrifying time.

Apparently, many other people from around the world are "making this up" too. It's so heartwarming to talk with people who tell their stories about discovering this for themselves. It's beautiful and precious, and there is an innocence to this discovery that I find speaks to my soul.

Chapter 6

People Are Waking Up

The best and most beautiful things in the world cannot be seen or even touched—
They must be felt with the heart.
~ Helen Keller

For the past seventy-five years or so, many people have not been part of caring for their own family members as they die, and they certainly have not been a part of caring for their own dead. But our present times are reflecting a shift in perspective over the last several years. An increasing number of people are questioning accepting every treatment that is offered to them; hospice services are becoming more understood and accepted; palliative care prior to hospice is something that is seen in many hospitals now; there is actually an association for home funerals in the United States; there are many talk about death platforms springing up all over (like Death Café); and several states in the United States have laws protecting assisted suicide. Yes, we are finally here—the baby boomers are dying, and they want choices.

Hospitals and undertakers handled our affairs regarding dying and death for most of the last century, and we willingly let them. Not so anymore. There is a growing trend in the United States of people wanting to regain control of caring for their own dying and dead. This is happening around the world.

Also, in the past ten years or so (since the 2000s), a disharmony has been growing between what people expect from hospice and what they receive. There are many reasons for this that I do not explore here. Just know that hospice services in the United States are being curtailed. Hospice professionals are forced to spend less time with families than they used to, employees' caseloads have significantly increased, and many people are talking about this. This trend is expected to continue. This is another reality that has fueled the end-of-life advocacy movement.

We are realizing that we may have given away more control than we wanted to at the end-of-life. People who are called to serve are seeing they would like to contribute to the present medical system and are finding ways to bridge services. They are seeing that our present system for tending to our dying needs help, and they want to be helpful.

An emerging energy of "advocacy" is growing in many people who want choices during illness and dying; they are no longer fighting death blindly at all costs. Patient advocacy is growing, as is awareness that palliative care is separate from hospice care. The World Health Organization defines palliative care in this way:

> *... Palliative care is an approach that improves the quality of life of patients and their families facing the problem associated with life-threatening illness, through the prevention and relief of suffering by means of early identification and impeccable assessment and treatment of pain and other problems, physical, psychosocial and spiritual....*

Palliative care should be planned and used concurrently with cure-directed treatment. In other words, palliative care is *not* just for the terminally ill. It is used for illnesses in addition to cancer, and it is used when you fully are expected to survive. It is *also* used by hospice as its sole method of care. That is one reason why people have mistakenly believed that hospice and palliative care are the same thing.

Palliative care can be a perfect bridge role to serve people as they move from expecting to recover to obtaining support for their dying, and at every "place of support" along the continuum from diagnosis through death.

There is a huge synergy now between our growing understanding (as a society) for empowerment regarding the way we die in modern times and the emerging end-of-life doula's desire to educate and serve. From my conversations with other death educators, we agree that the swell of people being called to serve is growing fast. Interestingly, they are being called to serve before the people who may need them are even conscious of them and their ability to help.

Chapter 7

Who Are These People, the Others Like *You*?

When you do things from your soul, you feel a river moving in you, a joy.
~ Jalaluddin Rumi

Even though I may talk to people every day who want to do this, I understand the calling is rare.

Think about all the people on the planet, and then think about how so many people avoid the subject of death and discussions on dying when it is their own approaching death or dying, and that of their family and friends. People tend to close down about this topic, although we are seeing an increase in people talking about death in places like Death Cafés and Death Over Dinner and other conversation platforms supporting these talks. But, for the most part, how many people do you know who feel it is negative to discuss it?

But people like me and you walk toward this discussion, even befriend it; we find joy in the thought of serving others, and we feel a deep happiness when we have accompanied another and have helped create a sacred circle at the end of life.

So, who are these people? They are not any one kind of person. Did you expect me to say that? Or did you think I was going to say they were of a certain type mostly?

If they each have something in common, it is this: all of them are very aware that there is fear for many people in this sacred transition and that they want to be part of relieving that. There is also a spiritual quality in each person I have ever spoken with that is shared regardless of individual religious and spiritual believe systems and teachings. That spiritual quality is they have a sense of themselves as a healing and grounding presence and that this presence does bring stability to another in their dying. They are comfortable with dying and death, respect it, and want to be a comforting, grounding presence for others and their families as they and their families engage with dying and death. We want to empower people to learn how to care for their own families through dying, reminding them of what they once knew.

They come from all religions and spiritual worldviews. From atheist to shaman, from fundamentalist Christian to Wiccan. They come from all educational backgrounds, from high school dropout to PhD. They come from all professions: barbers, bartenders, physicians, nurse practitioners, life coaches, certified nursing assistants, professors, acupuncturists, homemakers, psychotherapists, sales reps, organizational leaders, lawyers, and on and on.

They have one thing in common: they want to help bring light into the darkness of most of the Western world's fear about dying. They are pioneers in this, as there are few role models in our communities up to now. Most felt that they made it up in their own minds, and then they did a Google search and saw that there actually was such a thing as a "death doula," an "end-of-life doula," and so on. (In my case, though, when I thought I made it up and did a search back in 2005, I actually found *no one* on the internet searches who was end-of-life doula).

End-of-life doulas are people who want to serve others in a variety of ways—as a special focus in our area of expertise, as a volunteer and as their life's work, not just on weekends or after their eight-hour day at the office. They want to do this even though there is no promise of an income or riches or fame. They are spending their hard-earned money to learn about this art now when there is no "market" waiting for them. Most people are not conscious of end-of-life doula services.

Another reality is that end-of-life doulas are training to serve a community of individuals who do not acknowledge they are dying. The people who enroll with me understand that they are pioneers. On one hand, most people say that they *know* they will die, but on another level, most of us are shocked when it actually comes. To many it is negative thinking to talk about it or plan for it.

They are ready to go out into their communities to educate the public about the necessity for planning for their dying and death. They are fully aware that most people do not want to hear what they have to say. Most people actually feel that they have time to plan for their dying later.

But what is also true is that there is an awakening going on not only around the United States but also in other developed and developing countries around the world, for example, Canada, Australia, the United Kingdom, New Zealand, Ireland, and other countries, that we need to plan for our dying and death while we are healthy while no illness or situation is happening. We need to do this for very practical reasons, and we need to realize that facing our fears of dying and death will enable us to live a richer, more fulfilling life.

A depth of experience enters our lives when, as Reverend Bodhi Be says, "we realize we will die, we just don't know when or how." It means more to us to make sure we forgive, repair, reconcile, love, do what we want, mean what we say, and so on. Life has more richness, more depth, more breadth, and more love. So much more matters as the realization of our finite life on earth gives us a boundary that demands we pay attention to our heart and what we really want. Everything and everyone mean more.

So, these wonderful people like you and me are very dedicated, wanting to invest their energy, time, and money to help complete strangers die with grace and peace and less fear. The likelihood of hardship in starting their practice is not slowing them down. They are passionate about their calling. They tell me the most beautiful stories about how they knew they were meant to accompany others. I am proud to accompany them and grateful to be *their* guide.

Chapter 8

Accountants and Closet Organizers

As we let our own light shine, we unconsciously
give other people permission to do the same.
~ Marianne Williamson

Most people know that when it's time to pay their taxes and they feel they are in over their head and want help, there is a professional (an industry) there to help them. They know the name of this kind of role. It is called an accountant, bookkeeper, or tax professional, among others. A pathway has been established to be able to find help if you want it. The same thing happens if you have the money and need help with organizing. Most people know they can call someone to come organize their closets.

Most people have no idea that there is anyone who can help them as their loved one declines toward death. All they may know is that there are caregivers and companions (who may or may not be comfortable with dying and death).

Most people are not even conscious that there is a growing movement of people like us, much less know how to refer to us. People in this growing field are not even calling themselves the same things, even though they may be *doing* the same things. (See "Unity in the Movement: Tackling the Name of This Role," in the Supplemental Materials section.) There is even disagreement among the people who are serving privately at the end of life about what to call themselves. This is a very personal service, being created from the heart. People really want to identify with the title they call themselves, even though the role with a different title may be the same. It isn't simply a matter of telling them to "just call yourself a transition guide," for example. Maybe one day we will evolve to that, but I doubt it.

This is heart-centered service, not a medical role. This is a personal and community role and calling. This is mostly outside the system right now. The people who are doing it are fiercely independent and passionate about what is causing lack of adequate care, and they have their vision of what will make it better. This is not a combination that lends itself to easy consensus.

But they do seem to agree on one thing: They want to make the process of dying better for all of us, and they are seeking solutions that are not easily plugged in to the present system that they find broken. Many of them have come from the systems that they want to help repair. They have seen the gaps in health and death care and feel they cannot help within the system, so they choose to serve privately. They are choosing to serve outside of hospice, the hospitals, and the clinics. But that doesn't mean it is an adversarial role. In my training, I share my vision of our having an adjunctive role and an advocacy role with and within hospitals, hospices and other caregiving agencies, as well as the family. We help people and their families and we support them and their choices. We add stability to what can be a very difficult time. In this we are helping the system as well as the family.

The following list is just a few titles people are calling themselves in the role of "one who accompanies another through dying":

amicus
care doula
comfort care doula
deathsitter
deathwalker
death buddy
death coach
death doula
death guide
death midwife
doula for the dying
doula quietus
end-of-life doula
end-of-life midwife
end-of-life coach

griefwalker
midwife for the dying
soul doula
soul guide
soul midwife
transition coach
transition guide

Chapter 9

Hands-On Experience

A good head and a good heart are always a formidable combination.
~ Nelson Mandela

Know this: If you are a person who is called to this and have no experience with people dying, or if you only have a handful of experiences, then, to truly be helpful to others, you need to commit to being at the bedside of the dying and learning what it looks like, what people need, how you can be helpful, and how to care for yourself. You really need to know whether this is something real for you or may be something you are exploring for other reasons.

Exploring it is wonderful. But before you decide to create a practice, it is wise to put yourself in a position to learn as much as you can. Reading and doing exercises and discussing it all is one thing; "being there" is quite another. You are not going to be an equipped end-of-life doula after a weekend workshop with me or anyone else or even after months in my program unless you do one thing: gain your own personal experience. You need time with people at the bedside. That is what will solidify your calling. That experience is your best teacher.

I ask all my students to get hands-on experience with their local hospice and/or hospital. I supervise a practicum for them as well. It is so important. Sometimes the calling you have is not going to be about creating a practice for your community. Sometimes this pull toward the topic of death and dying is to explore your own mortality. Most people in your circle will look at this as strange because many do everything they can to separate themselves from their inevitable death. But no one cheats death. No one.

So isn't it interesting that in order to be in the company of those who understand you, the one who is called to explore your own mortality, you cannot simply talk to your neighbor or friend about it; you must talk to people deeply called to serve others? This shows how disconnected we are as a society from the fact that we all will die a certain death; we just don't know how, and we don't know when.

Sometimes, a person will have this deep desire to know more so that he may serve his own family and friends through life and be the go-to person. Think of how beautiful that is, to be part of the dying of the people you love the most. You will be responsible for empowering the people you love the most in learning how to care for their own families and neighbors. This exploration will give meaning and depth to everyone whose life you touch. It empowers you *and* everyone you serve. Usually someone is watching at all times when I'm serving a family. Someone wants to learn the ways of "one who accompanies."

Chapter 10

Outside the System

Your time is limited, so don't waste it living someone else's life.
Don't be trapped by dogma—which is living with the results of other people's thinking.
Don't let the noise of other's opinions drown out your own inner voice.
And most important, have the courage to follow your heart and intuition.
~ Steve Jobs

The first wave of people called to bring peace to the dying, separate from those who never stopped knowing (our grandmothers and grandfathers and people who knew how to care for the ill and dying within the family), were members of what we know now as the hospice and palliative care movement led by Dame Cicely Saunders, Balfour Mount, and the like. The movement started outside of the medical establishment at the time by someone inside of it.

It called on the grassroots power of people interested in making a difference, and we see how powerful this has been. Hospice has been incorporated into the United States Medicare system. In the United States, palliative-care practitioners and programs are working on finding ways to finance palliative care. It is not completely covered at this time. Palliative care funding is very inconsistent across America. In other countries around the world, such as Canada and England, it is different. Nowhere is it perfect.

Learning to die in present times naturally (dying organically) is in its infancy; as we are dealing with dying under different circumstances in the history of the earth, we are dying in different times. We are dying slowly, with chronic diseases, living with advanced illness for many years before death. We used to not live with illness for so long. The question now is, "How do we die now, in this day and age?" We are just beginning to come to our senses after decades believing we could fight death and win.

Over the last forty years or so, people have been channeling their passion to serve the dying through the hospice movement. And just like everything organizational and medical, there are gaps in care in hospice services having mostly to do with time. People have experienced it and want to do something about filling the need. People serving in roles within hospice, paid and unpaid, talk about wanting to "do more," to serve "beyond hospice."

As with any organization, there are rules within it to be obeyed and boundaries to uphold to maintain stability. Every system has strengths and weaknesses. In the United States, much of the interest in this new wave of end-of-life support is because of people responding to the gaps they are still seeing in care. They want to keep improving the model.

Also, we still have the unavailability of hospice services to so many people around the world, even in 2016, even in the United States, for one of the richest countries in the world. According to the latest statistics, only 45 percent of people in the United States die utilizing hospice services. There are still people who don't know much about it and that they can utilize it, or they fear it and don't *want* to use it. Some people even believe that hospice services are an attempt to *not* give superior services to a certain class of people, that medical professionals are giving up on them and offering them a less-expensive and lesser alternative, or that hospice is part of a system to "not save their life."

So around the world, support for the dying is inconsistent, and where it has been utilized well, there may be holes in the service. The initial wave of death support via hospice in the late 1960s set the stage for what we are now improving on. Baby boomers are aging. The talk-about-death movement really began to take over the world in 2011 (when Death Café took its first steps; see www.deathcafe.com). In the United States, the questions now are, "How do you do it? How do you take care of your own dying?" These questions are being asked all over the world.

Chapter 11

Hospice and the End-of-Life Doula

When your love and skill work together, expect a masterpiece.
~ John Ruskin

Until now, most of the people doing this work were paid professionals within the hospice organization and volunteers. There are several roles open for people who choose to do their death work there: physician, nurse, social worker, chaplain, certified nursing assistant, volunteer, and bereavement counselor. I am assisting progressive hospices now in building end-of-life doula programs, so there is a new role emerging within hospice: the end-of-life doula volunteer. (The end-of-life doula programs are more involved than just the "eleventh hour" or vigil programs.)

This new role within hospices for the end-of-life doula supports hospices in key areas and bridges hospice services not only leading to the hours before death but to the entire pre- and post-death period. There is also the need for people to find meaning in their lives. The "legacy" movement in end-of-life circles answers this need. You will hear it be referred to as an "ethical will" or "legacy work." This work is also incorporated into the end-of-life doula role within hospices.

The role of end-of-life doula is ideal for bridging this area at a point when hospice seems to lack time. As the doula gets to know the family, he or she is also gathering information for the vigil time and for documenting the person's legacy.

The doula also spends significant time with an individual during imminent death if the family wishes it. Also, I recommend the end-of-life doula to make at least 1 of 2 bereavement visits. If so, then the doula becomes a beautiful role within hospice that helps to bridge the gaps in death care *within the hospice,* providing continuity of care at the end of life, from hospice entry through bereavement. In hospice circles we hear the misunderstandings and hurt feelings from families that they feel they were dropped at the death of their loved one, that the whole team was suddenly gone. As much as we prepare them for this, it's still shocking and hurtful sometimes. An end of life doula who begins visits with the team and continues on after death may be helpful in soothing this for families.

Chapter 12

The Independent End-of-Life Doula

Passion will move men beyond themselves,
beyond their shortcomings,
beyond their failures.
~ Joseph Campbell

If you are presently involved in the death empowerment movement, you have surely noticed the creative new services being offered. People are doing living wakes, bedside singing, end-of-life planning, and end-of-life concierge. There are celebrants and ritualists. There are palliative advocates, shamans, death coaches, soul midwives, and many other roles.

A growing number of individuals are offering a variety of creative services in response to people's desire to take control of their life, illness, dying, death, and interment.

We have learned that green burial is better for the environment than cremation. We are learning we can have ocean burials. We are learning we can have home funerals and home burials. There is so much developing relating to the end-of-life. It coincides with the baby boomers' coming into their old age and dying.

I founded an organization called the End-of-life Practitioners Collective (ELPC). Please visit www.endoflifepro.org to join us if you are a person who serves others in independent practice in your community. People need us and have no idea how to find us. We make it hard on them by calling ourselves various titles and only being listed in the schools we studied under or on our own personal websites. Hopefully, this will help people be able to find the support they need when they need it. For years, people have said to me, "I wish I had known about you and people like you when I was going through this." The ELPC concept is unique in that the practitioners have a place to find each other, refer to each other, and collaborate, and consumers have a place to find someone to help them in a variety of ways. Please spread the word.

Chapter 13

One Phone Call

Each one of us can make a difference. Together we make change.
~ Barbara Mikulski

We can never know the outcome of any of our moves. We don't know how people will respond to us, ever. All we can do is come from the highest place inside of us and take action.

In the planning for my training for the International Death Doula Conference in April 2017 in Maui, organized by Doorway into Light, I had a thought one afternoon. I saw there was some confusion about what is going on in the end-of-life doula movement as my email was blowing up after a recent article.

My thought was, "Call the NHPCO (National Hospice and Palliative Care Organization) and talk to someone." So, I did.

I phoned our national trade group of hospices, the largest and oldest trade group for hospice and palliative care, the NHPCO. It had been on my mind that they would be perfect to speak with to see how all these amazing doulas from all the training programs could be helpful to them.

When I called, one person led to another and I found myself speaking with John Mastrojohn, COO of NHPCO, and what a delightful conversation that was. He thought it was a great idea too for us to have further conversations. I sent him a list of end-of-life educators who trained laypeople and healthcare professionals in end of life care, regardless of what they called themselves. He invited us all for a talk in San Diego that September at the Management and Leadership Conference.

Those who responded and were present for that meeting with me were Tarron Estes of Conscious Dying; Merilynne Rush, RN of Lifespan Doula Association; Patty Burgess-Brecht of Teaching Transitions/Doing Death Differently; Trudy Brown, an assistant to Patty; Suzanne O'Brien, RN of Doulagivers; from the NHPCO, John Mastrojohn, COO; Edo Banach, CEO; and Beth Fells, Executive Office Director in NHPCO.

We discussed the movement now, history that led us here and visions for the future. We discussed how we could possibly help hospices and palliative care organizations and what would be the best way to bring the talent we were seeing as trainers to the industry. Then there was the *after-meeting* meeting. And at *that* meeting, the idea of what we know now as the National End-of-Life Doula Alliance (NEDA) was born.

At our second meeting with NHPCO staff in Alexandria, Virginia, in November 2017, John surprised us with a beautiful idea. He told us he would ask the board if it would be in NHPCO's best interest to create a council for end-of-life doulas, where we could educate their member hospices and palliative-care organizations, as well as consumers, about us and how we could be helpful to them. We were all ecstatic and so grateful! At this meeting with me were Lee Webster, a pioneering end of life educator and advocate, Henry Fersko-Weiss, Janie Rakow and Jerri Glatter of INELDA, Patty Burgess-Brecht of Teaching Transitions, and Suzanne O'Brien of Doulagivers, along with John Mastrojohn and Beth Fells from the NHPCO.

On February 7, 2018, I received a phone call. I missed it but when I saw the name on the call, I immediately listened to the voice mail (I still have it today). That is the day Beth called me to say the board approved the End-of-Life Doula Advisory Council.

A new day was born for end-of-life doulas. We have been working hard for this. The great connection was beginning. The connection was between a pool of highly passionate people who wanted to be supportive in non-medical, innovative ways, with the service providers who presently needed help providing services to the dying. These end of life doulas are becoming a powerful bridge and adjunct to our present health care systems.

Don't ever underestimate the power of one action of yours. There are many people all over the world who want to do the same thing we are doing; they want to help and be a part of the solution of dying well in the modern age. All that I described earlier happened because many people said yes! John said yes to me, and everyone who has played a role since then said yes to him and to everyone involved.

Who will say "yes!" to you?

PART II

How to Accompany the Dying

As an end-of-life doula, you may feel a real draw to help people all along the continuum, from wellness to bereavement. You may feel a special draw to a specific period within a lifetime, or you may want to engage with all the periods.

I believe the doula role is excellent during every life phase. We are very familiar with it during the birthing phase. And most of us know there are guides—consultants or coaches—for when we marry or for when we want a more fulfilling life or career. But what about the other major transitions? It is okay to bring the doula role to all phases as we transition, not just during the end of life. In this book however, we will stay focused on the end-of-life period.

Chapter 14

Where Do We Begin?

It's never crowded along the extra mile.
~ Wayne Dyer

As an end-of-life doula, where will you begin your walk with people? Do you just want to focus on the period of imminent dying? During the days and hours leading to death and the hours and days afterward? Do you want to be a part of assisting people prior to this time, when they are declining (prior to hospice services) and not doing well in the process?

Or do you want to educate and accompany people when they get a diagnosis, early in the process of an illness, to help them manage it all? Do you want to educate about death and dying and advance directives while people are healthy and having a great time, to help them see that engaging with their dying during these years will have the best outcome for everyone? Do you want to guide people during post-death vigil (as a home funeral guide) and/or home burials? Do you want to offer bereavement companionship, regardless of what else you do?

Are you a practitioner of other healing modalities who wants to add end-of-life services to your menu? Are you the go-to person, the someone to whom everyone comes when something "bad" happens or when someone is dying? Are you the one who knows the end of life very well and wants to share your wisdom and serve your community privately? Are you working within an organization and looking to create an end-of-life service or program within it?

In this book, I will share how to accompany the dying. But first it's important for you to decide where you want to begin your walk with someone. I will address helping others in each period.

Chapter 15

When All Is Well

Each night, when I go to sleep, I die.
And the next morning, when I wake up, I am reborn.
~ Mahatma Gandhi

Do you really know that at this *very moment* you are not in the early stages of an aggressive cancer that will wait to surface until you are nearly dead? I'm not trying to be negative; this sometimes happens. And are you sure you are not going to fall down the stairs and be brain-dead for the rest of your life? Or won't have a car accident that leaves you unresponsive? You cannot know, can you?

How do we get each other to see that this is true—that we will all die, and that we don't know when or how? We need to buy in to the fact that if we actually think and plan for our dying and death, it will be best for ourselves and our families. It won't make it happen sooner (I've been talking about it for twenty years now); it will enable the process to be a smoother experience when it does happen. And it will.

If you want to engage with people who are healthy now, who are not facing serious issues presently, one way to do that is to have some fun with how you deliver your message. Humor always goes a long way, and especially with this group. Remember, many people are death-phobic—very uncomfortable with death and dying—and a lot of nervous giggling is prone to happen anyway. Take advantage of this.

Where do you have connections with people happily engaged in life? Experiential seminars and half-days would be perfect if you want to get people's attention. Because people in this crowd aren't actively engaging with their own dying at the moment, you can be more outrageous with your seminars, retreats, workshops, or whatever you have up your sleeve.

Or you can approach this in seriousness. See about arranging a workshop with people who are dying, who may want to share their experiences with those who aren't. This would be real instruction in how they are facing their dying. Or, you could do a documentary project and share it with others. Ask your local hospice if it knows of any people who would like to be interviewed about what it is like to die and how they are handling it.

There are so many possibilities.

As an end-of-life doula, part of your practice could be to engage with people here, in the prime of their lives. It is the perfect time, and many people are called to educate at this time. You can always facilitate a discussion; you don't have to be an expert to do that. If you want to talk about a certain topic, please make sure you speak on subjects in which you are well versed, or you could host subject-matter experts in your community.

As a leader in end-of-life care in your community, you want to be a part of empowering and educating your community about why it is important to plan now, while they are healthy and life is pretty good, and show the benefits of doing so.

Why we should plan now:
> It's less emotionally painful.
> You have a chance to have your wishes fulfilled. Remember: We will all die, we just don't know when and how. Some people will linger needlessly even though they are dying or technically "dead" because these decisions were not made or known ahead of time.
> You are a role model for taking responsibility for one's life and death. You will be an inspiration for others to do the same.
> You are relieving your family of the burden of tremendous guilt. If you have a plan they can follow, they will not be placed in the predicament of having to make your decisions for you.
> It's the kindest gift you can give to the people you love.

Key Points for the "All Is Well" Stage:
1. Provide discussion time for family, friends, and community members about dying, death, advance directives, and issues surrounding the end-of-life.
2. When people are in good health, it is not as threatening to discuss and complete advance directives and funeral and burial plans.

3. Have small parties or gatherings to address specific issues and explore people's thoughts.
4. Have your own advance directives completed and your own funeral and burial plans completed. You don't have to purchase anything, but know where you want to go and whom you want to use.

Chapter 16

Early in the Process of Illness
(Until Treatments Begin to Stop Working)

The fear of death follows from the fear of life.
A man who lives fully is prepared to die at any time.
~ Mark Twain

You may be an end-of-life doula or practitioner who will also accompany people during the illness process. This is a perfect role for people who have a strong advocacy edge to their practice already or in the way they envision their practice.

Whether the person has been diagnosed as terminal or is fully expected to live, to accompany him or her during this very uncertain time, fraught with tremendous anxiety and soul-searching, remaining unattached to their feelings about treatment—whether mainstream, alternative, or something else—is extremely helpful during this time.

This is where many ill people feel overwhelmed and lost. They may be facing the fear of their own death for the first time. Regardless of their age, this is very disorienting. Everything a person has believed and built his or her life on until now is usually brought into question. He or she is in crisis of survival. Even if a cancer diagnosis is "minor," the word *cancer* usually brings people to the brink of their own death in their mind.

Also, there can be many gaps in healthcare delivery at this time, depending on your service provider and city services. Even though insurance companies and hospitals are developing new roles, such as "navigators," for example, many people in the system report feeling lost and afraid. They feel that they are not receiving consistent information.

If you want to assist people during this time, learn all you can about palliative care (non-hospice) programs in your area and acquaint yourself with "alternative modalities" that may help with symptom management, for example, acupuncture, chiropractic, reiki, aromatherapy, therapeutic massage, and so on; learn about people offering emotional and spiritual support for various conditions.

A spiritually based practice of accompanying people in finding meaning during this time would be perfect—doing legacy projects, reconciling with family and friends, and so forth. So would a practice that assists with practical matters, especially helping people with their medical bills and insurance claims. These activities are daunting for most people.

A patient-advocacy practice would be perfect for people who know the medical system quite well, regardless of how you acquired the knowledge. You don't have to be a medical professional to be great at it. You have to be resourceful, know your way around healthcare somewhat, and be willing to do a lot of legwork for a family. It is also worthwhile to consider professional patient-advocacy programs.

The main thing to remember is that as a doula, you are walking alongside a person and his or her family. Do not get caught up in believing you have to give advice. Unless you are an expert in an area the person needs help with, you should not be offering advice. You can be a companion, help them with practical chores, make sure things are getting accomplished, do research for them, and help them at appointments and with insurance-company paper trails.

Also, this is a perfect time for legacy projects. People facing their own mortality are usually seriously contemplating what is meaningful for them. Many describe this time as a period of deep transformation. It is the perfect time to assist them with a project that may encapsulate what has given their life meaning up to now and what they see for the generations to come. It would be a great time for a project of some sort, for example, an ethical will, an oral history, video interviews, and/or a written project. Not only will this be deeply meaningful for them should they survive this time, but also it will help them process their emotions.

Whatever you choose to do, make sure it is something you feel confident in engaging in, that you know what you are talking about, that you have the necessary credentials or background, and that you do not misrepresent yourself in any way. *Do not stretch the truth. You do not need to be an expert to be a companion.*

During this time, some of the people you serve will die quickly or unexpectedly. Usually, at the beginning of a diagnosis with a serious illness, regardless of how dire, people are raring to fight it and have hope that they will be the miracle case. Of course, sometimes the person will die "unexpectedly." Sometimes, especially during treatments for cancer, for instance, someone can come very close to death or appear as though he or she is actually in the dying process. If you are working with these people at the time, it is important to bring their attention to having their affairs in order, just in case they have times when they are unable to speak for themselves. Advocating for this process is the kindest thing you can do for that person and his or her family.

If the person is dying, you will most likely see this as it is happening. The person and/or the family may be unwilling to see it. You can still be instrumental during this time because you may be able to offer suggestions or a direction that could help make this period more peaceful, even if everyone is unable or unwilling to admit the person is dying. Be proactive with getting assistance, resources, and options ready so that the person or his or her primary caregiver is able to take action before the last minute. You must use your discernment about when and how to address the fact that dying may be what is happening right now and that preparing for it is the next best thing to do so that the person has the best chance to die well and leave his or her loved ones in the best possible position.

Although it is not your job or responsibility to make decisions for them or to tell them what to do, it is within your role to have options available and thoughts of people who may be able to help. Get to know people within a palliative care practice and within hospice to call on quickly. Know that to get into a palliative care practice, usually a referral from the person's primary care physician is required. It takes time for that office to get records sent to the palliative practice and for the palliative physician to review them and accept the case. It is important to get this referral in place as soon as it becomes evident you may need it. Some practitioners will not even consider a person unless his or her symptoms are severe or unmanageable. Find out about the referral process in your town.

So many people after the death of a loved one describe a nightmarish time of transition from health to dying. They report that they, and most people in the circle around the person, had no idea what was going on. At least, with you present, *there is a chance for so much to go right, even if it is the person's time to die.*

Key Points for "Early in the Process":

1. Know the palliative care options in your town. Know the physicians, clinics, and hospitals in your town that have a non-hospice palliative-care team or program. They may be called "supportive care" or "advanced illness management."

2. Have a contact within a hospice whom you trust who respond to you quickly. There are times when a person's health may quickly decline and the physicians on the case do not believe a hospice referral is warranted, but the person who is dying would like to talk to hospice. Have your contact within hospice call and let him or her figure out how to get this discussion scheduled as quickly as possible. Chances are the person and his or her family are overwhelmed, and the hospital or doctor you are dealing with may not be savvy in end-of-life matters or even in recognizing that a person is actually dying.

3. Practice deep listening; do not talk or advise, as much as you may feel the impulse to do so. People need to work out their own issues, and they need a lot of room to do that. They are working out their life; most of the time, they simply need a loving witness. If they need advice, let them be the one to ask you for it. Err on the side of *no advice*.

4. Practical help may be the biggest thing you can offer here.

5. Help the person with a legacy project.

6. If you see that dying is happening quickly and no one seems to be acting on this fact, address the most reasonable person in the family system and ask that family member what he or she sees is happening. Ask, "If, in fact, [name] is dying, would you want more support than you are now receiving? Are you willing to talk to the physician about a hospice referral? Do you want me with you?" Be prepared to walk the family member through admittance to hospice service if it is appropriate.

Chapter 17

Advanced Illness Decline (Prior to Hospice)

Every breath you take, you are getting closer to the grave.
But every breath you take, you can also get closer to your liberation.
~ Sadhguru

By the time of the end-stage illness and advanced illness, so much has happened in trying to heal and recover to full functioning. So much hope is already gone for things ever being the way they were prior to the illness. People are now looking for a relief from suffering and are trying to "stay on top" of their illness or to stay as fully functioning as possible. Unless the person is diagnosed "terminal," and even if someone is diagnosed terminal, there may be much hope of recovery or a return to some prior level of functioning. Often, though, people are truly trying to keep what they presently have, and they have hope for a longer life than is being projected.

We understand this, don't we? It is a rare person who takes this stage in stride and realizes that he or she is declining toward death and does not fight it. Many people die during this time without the support of hospice. A lot of dying in this period is stressful, scary, chaotic, and disempowering for the person and family. There is much confusion in medical circles also about how to deal with people during this time. There is so much disparity in the training of medical professionals relating to this time. In short, this is a hard time for *everyone* to navigate in and out of medical circles.

But we count on the medical profession to guide us in healthcare. Yes, we do. And in death care, we count on hospice to guide us. But what about the time in between? What about this middle ground between "doing everything" and "doing nothing"?

Let's talk about this time of when everyone involved understands that we are not at the beginning, and we are not at the end at this moment, but we are definitely moving toward dying. Let's assume, for the purpose of our discussion, the people involved feel that death is possible "in the next year or so." Many people actually live for years with "end-stage" illness diagnoses. Also, many people die during this time and are caught unprepared.

You may begin to hear the word *terminal* and the word *hospice*. The words *end-stage illness* or *advanced illness* may be uttered. Perhaps "incurable" is stated. In reality, most physicians refer people to hospice way too late in the dying process. Understand that just because a person does not receive a hospice referral, it does not mean they are not dying. Only 45 percent of people die on hospice, according to the latest statistics gathered (2015 NHPCO Facts and Figures: Hospice Care in America reported total number of estimated hospice deaths in 2014 as 1,200,000 and the Centers for Disease Control reported total deaths in the United States in 2014 as 2,626,418). That means there is a whole lot of dying happening outside of hospice. And most of that "dying on hospice" is happening during the last week or so of life (according to the preceding study from the NHPCO). In other words, most of the dying prior to imminent death is happening without hospice support.

Do you see why it may be one of the most rewarding and challenging roles, to be a guide during this time as well? It is a different part of the healthcare system. Being a doula as an adjunct within the hospice model of care is really different than being a doula within the acute care model of care, even if the person is at the same exact point in their dying process. Your role as an end-of-life doula is to be an advocate of sorts in both realms, but if the person is still in the acute care system, you will be seen as more of a healthcare advocate as well as an emotional and spiritual companion.

People are usually still open to trying new things during this time, especially if they are still suffering and have not had adequate palliative care. Introduce palliative care to them if they have not experienced it. If they are not suffering physically, let them know about it, begin to do your search for it in your area, and get it on the radar in case issues begin to arise. Don't wait for a crisis.

Many people during this period have exacerbations of their illness and are making frequent hospital trips. Again, palliative care is the only method of care that will minimize this insanity. Find out who is the best at managing symptoms of the sort experienced by the person you are helping. Ask the person if he or she wants to continue hospitalizations, what has his or her physician said about the trajectory of the illness, whether anyone has mentioned hospice to him or her, and other questions that will help you get clear about what they need.

If the person you are helping has not completed advance directives, this needs to be addressed. Help him or her complete the paperwork. Help facilitate a family meeting if needed to let everyone know who will matter at that time what the client wants and where the papers are.

In advanced illness and end-stage illness, some people are actually in the dying process and not receiving hospice services. They are going in and out of the hospital, and no one is conscious of the fact or addressing the fact the person is dying. You may be able to see it, and no one in the medical system has addressed it. If you see this, talk to the person who is ill and ask what he or she feels is happening. So many times, they know what is happening and keep it to themselves because there is no one they feel safe with to talk to about it.

This is an unfortunate truth, but one you must know: the present healthcare system does not support the time it takes to deal with people who are dying, especially people who are transitioning into the terminal status. It takes time to "have the talk" with someone you realize is actually in the dying process and not just "sick with the flu." More than a few physicians have told me that unfortunately, they did not have the time it takes to deal with these discussions, *and they knew it at the time.*

So people should not assume that just because no one has discussed hospice or dying with them, they are not dying. It may be as simple as the fact that no one has the time to talk about it. It may be that the present team of professionals is not well trained for this talk or is uncomfortable with it. Do not assume that all healthcare professionals are good at every phase of healthcare delivery. They are not. That's why there are specialties.

When people fully understand that they are in advanced illness or end-stage illness, they usually understand they will not return to their prior, pre-illness level of functioning.

Talk to them and see if they want to talk with their primary caregiver and family about what is happening now, especially if you can clearly see they are moving toward their death and nothing has been addressed thus far. Find out if they would like help from a close friend, chaplain, or professional to help with this talk. There may be great emotion at the onset of the discussion, but you will be helping them get their affairs in order and helping them have their wishes fulfilled while there is still time.

It is not the ideal time to get a person's affairs in order, but it is better than having a crisis-driven death. The best time to get affairs in order, directives complete, and a vigil plan in place is when everything is fine, when the person's health is great. But sometimes, nothing is done until right before death—this is still better than having *no* support.

Chances are if you are meeting someone who wants your help at this time and is not on hospice, you may be helping them sign up with a hospice service during your time with them. Learn all you can about hospice and about the hospices in your area.

If you see that people clearly transitioning into dying are not on hospice, your role here is to find out from the person, if he or she is still conscious, what the person wants. Does he or she want to die a natural death, supported by hospice and his or her family in peace? Does he or she want to try every means imaginable to stay alive? You can find out by asking him or her directly, *"If someone should walk into your room and your heart has stopped beating, do you want extreme measures used to revive you?"* If the answer is "No, I want to be let go naturally and peacefully," begin to take steps to bring hospice into the situation. If the answer is "Yes, I want to try every imaginable thing to stay alive," you know the person wants to go to the hospital when symptoms are severe.

If the person does not have good palliative care and is dying without hospice, his or her symptoms may become severe. Some people may decline peacefully. As a doula, it is your role during this period and in this setting to know of palliative-care consultation options, know the client's preference for natural death or extreme measures, and know and observe your boundaries.

Key Points for "Advance Illness" Stage (prior to hospice):
1. Know where the family stands regarding hospice service.
2. Make sure that the person and the family know that suffering is not par for the course and that the person doesn't have to be dying to be comfortable. Palliative medicine is possible prior to hospice. See "Palliative Care" in the Supplemental Materials section for a discussion on palliative care.
3. Find the palliative physicians, programs, clinics, and hospitals in your town that have excellent palliative services for people who are not on hospice.
4. Get to know someone in hospice whom you can call if the family wants hospice and the physician is unwilling to refer the person. Let the hospice handle the matter; its employees are used to these situations.

Chapter 18

The Decision for Hospice

A dying man needs to die, as a sleepy man needs to sleep,
And there comes a time when it is wrong, as well as useless, to resist.
~ Stewart Alsop

We want to be part of creating the reality for most people that the decision to going on hospice service is one that is not made in crisis. As of 2018, more people than not tend to decide to go on hospice service due to an "emergency."

The emergency is usually that the person is dying, and this person and the family are finally being referred to hospice in this dramatic state. Either the physician has not recommended the person come soon enough or the person and/or the family has not accepted the person's dying and has refused to begin hospice service. It is either one of these scenarios or a combination of both that creates the crisis decision to go on hospice service.

Let's dream for a minute. What would it be like if the person with an advanced illness were getting great palliative care the whole time he or she was receiving cure-directed treatments? What would it be like if the whole family were being treated in a palliative care program as well? Imagine that the person's symptoms have been well managed as he or she seeks to be cured, and the person's family has been receiving great emotional and spiritual support as well. This would be called great palliative care.

Then, at some point, it becomes evident that any cure-directed treatments will be futile and will only harm, not help, the person. So now, we are going to drop only the treatments that will add injury to the situation; we will continue the excellent palliative care. Now we are not in crisis because of unmanageable symptoms and scurrying to get on hospice at the eleventh hour. Instead, we are making a logical decision based on the situation; we are realizing that hospice is the next best step because there is no treatment to cure that will be acceptable at this point. It may be sad, of course, but it is not a crisis.

This is what we are aiming for: to make the decision for entry in to hospice service as "the next right step." To permit the adrenaline and fear on the part of someone dying in an uncontrolled series of medical events is unconscionable. We all need to do our part to stop this insanity. We all have a part in it. The person and family being affected are least responsible because they are usually the most uninformed, the most personally involved, and the most emotional about what is happening. We in the medical field, along with the doula, can be instrumental in recognizing a decline in a person's functioning and health and ensuring that excellent palliative care is being given as this decline occurs, to minimize the amount of hospitalizations, suffering, and emotional distress. When the person and his or her family are being expertly cared for, they are less likely to have uncontrolled anxiety infused in all their daily activities.

It is paramount that we all get better at recognizing and accepting that when a person's health and functioning are declining because of advanced illness, he or she is not going to magically be cured and restored to the health of a year or two ago or even of six months ago. We need to realize that we are dealing with a person who is declining toward eventual death. It may happen slowly, or it may happen quickly (for example, heart attack, stroke, or accident).

People who do not accept their dying. People may know that they are declining in health, never to regain prior functioning, yet still do not accept that death is coming. They may want to live, even if all they can move are their eyelids. How to support them best is to make sure they have the best palliative care possible and adjust everything you can to their level of present strength. Utilize the services of an occupational therapist to get ideas on how to accommodate anything they want to do to fit their present level of functioning.

They may never want to get on hospice services. That is fine as long as they are not suffering. Have the conversation with them that hospice knows how to deal with comfort better than any other branch of medicine, and the hospice service can always be fired if it is not serving you well. Explain that if their condition stabilizes, they will need to come off hospice service, and many people end up doing just that. Explain that hospice not only is *not* a certain death sentence but also can actually *extend* life. Please see the article in the *Journal of Pain and Symptom Management*, "Comparing Hospice and Nonhospice Patient Survival Among Patients Who Die Within a Three-Year Window."

People who will not accept their dying state *and* who qualify for hospice can still benefit from the great care hospice provides, if they are willing to give it a try. Just let the hospice know to follow the patient's lead (which the staff are trained to do). Tell them exactly how you want them to talk to the ill person and the family. They will oblige.

People who accept their dying. This is so much easier on everyone. People who are dying should be cared for by the best we have to offer. Hospice is the best all-around provider of care possible for those who are dying. There are other supports, of course — "alternative" health practitioners, with powerful healing modalities and treatments — but hospice should be the go-to source for expert care when people are dying.

Hospice is set up to care not only for the person who is dying but also for the family. They are organized to help the family on every level that is acknowledged in allopathic medicine: body, mind, and spirit. Hospice and other Western death-care providers do not usually address people's "energy system" or "energy body"; they are not addressing people on the energetic level. See your alternative practitioner — ayurvedic practitioner, acupuncturist, shaman, or other healer if you want this level of support.

The bottom line regarding hospice discussion is, take advantage of talking to several hospices the *first* time it is mentioned by your healthcare team. There is no reason to wait. You will receive excellent information to weigh into your decision-making. The hospice representatives will spend a lot of time with you. Get all the facts and "the rest of the story." So much of the time, you will hear from doctors and other medical professionals about treatment options spoken hurriedly, but you may not be hearing the repercussions of how life will be from those treatment options. That is what I call "the rest of the story." Hospice has the rest of the story, the complete story, of what life can be like if you quit fighting your death.

By advocating for hospice sooner, you are helping your clients see the wisdom in at least talking with someone who will spend a lot of time with them, helping them to get the full picture of their situation and sharing knowledge of their options. Most of what is happening right now is that families do not have all the information and that they are not getting much time with people who have great information. Hospice has great information.

I have seen more suffering from people fighting their death than I have from people who have accepted their death and had their symptoms managed well. Hospice does this better than anyone. And, if a loved one or client should end up on hospice services and not like the services he or she is receiving, you can call and tell the supervisor to fix whatever is wrong. The hospice will do its best. You can switch hospice companies if the problem isn't resolved.

It is *clearly* understood that most people do not want to die: "It is not the right time." "I'm not ready." "I want to [see one more thing, do one more thing, live one more day]." It is sad. It hurts the heart. Everyone understands why people avoid it.

As a doula, you will walk alongside a family, offering compassionate, loving care and advocacy at the appropriate times. How do you know if the time is appropriate? By taking care of yourself—mind, body, and spirit, emotionally and energetically. In this way, you will be more grounded and present and have better discernment. When you take great care of yourself, you can better trust your intuition. Many delicate conversations can be had with great finesse if you are well cared for and know how to have these conversations. Do not attempt to have delicate conversations with people if you have not been trained to do so, or if you do not have a natural gift for talking to people about difficult situations.

Key Points for a "Decision for Hospice":
1. If a physician recommends hospice service, *do* encourage people to take the time to talk to at least one hospice company and gather information. They will be glad they did. Hospice offers great advice and new ways to look at the situation.
2. Know that not all hospices give great service (just like in any other industry). If the family is unhappy, let the provider know that they do not have to endure substandard service. Call management to get the problem resolved; and if they must, they can change hospice providers. Most hospices will do all they can to handle any matter that should arise.
3. It is better to get into hospice service sooner rather than later. If the person stabilizes, he or she can always come off hospice service and be discharged. People live longer while in hospice service, and hospice provides many wonderful advantages.
4. As a doula, you are part of the care team. Do all you can to be helpful to hospice. If you see something amiss, don't inflate the problem with the family or point it out if they haven't noticed. Call the hospice and let the registered nurse case manager know what is going on so that he or she can fix the problem. Be part of "soothing and smoothing." Help the hospice give great service while you are part of calming the family. Do not agitate; instead, help to dissipate anger. Many people project their frustrations onto

issues other than the fact that someone they love with all their heart is dying. Anything you can do to keep peace will enhance the experience for the family. We are part of minimizing drama.

Chapter 19

End Days: Person on Hospice

Death is not the greatest loss in life.
The greatest loss is what dies inside us while we live.
~ Norman Cousins

When people are receiving hospice services, the ideal situation is that they have a fantastic hospice service and that they and their family have most of their needs met adequately to superbly, and everything goes well.

Even if the hospice is stellar, there is still much to do to help the daily activity of tending to the dying go as smoothly as possible. It is amazing how many people are required to keep one dying person well cared for. If you consider the primary caregiver in the mix, it takes more of the village. We all should consider the primary caregiver, but he or she is often neglected. Do your absolute best to help meet the primary caregiver's needs. It is amazing how many caregivers care for their dying loved one with little to no help. Most people do not have an ever-present large family to help. Support primary caregivers as they tend to their loved one as he or she die.

Keep in mind that hospice is *not* a caregiving organization; it is a consulting organization that also offers certified nursing assistants who will come one to five days per week, as needed, to help bathe the dying person and do light housekeeping when the person is sleeping. The family must arrange for their own daily caregiving needs. They cannot leave the house when hospice comes to get their errands done or take a break. The primary caregiver or someone else must be there.

You can be instrumental in organizing the incoming requests by neighbors and friends to serve the family. Use an online community such as Careflash, one of the best in the industry, to keep it all organized. Help the family hire caregivers, and help them with the practical needs of the day. Help them assess the last wishes of the dying person. Help make any forgiveness experiences happen, or help with anything that could be weighing heavily on anyone in the family. Use the hospice's resources as much as possible. The people working in hospice want to be helpful, and they want to know what is going on. Make sure you speak with the family and ask them if you can share with the hospice case manager what you are observing so that hospice can be well informed on how to best help the family.

The hospice will handle everything to do with the death and disposition of the body. If the family is not taking advantage of all the hospice has to offer, encourage them to do so. Hospice is here to make this time easier. Let them.

If the family has had the good fortune to get on to hospice services long before the imminent death of their loved one, this time has the greatest chance of being peaceful. So many unexpected things can occur, though, that could make this a very trying time; for example, symptoms could become difficult to manage, family members may have emotional turmoil, and outside events may affect the environment of the dying person in some way. Many things could come up, and your hospice will be or should be ready to help in every instance.

Key Point for "End Days" (person on hospice service):
> Encourage communication between the family and hospice. Help to build trust and confidence. It will help the family feel better overall to trust their hospice. If there are issues big enough to not warrant trust like this, then management must be called and be given the opportunity to make it right, or another hospice should be called in. The dying person deserves the best care possible at this time. Be part of making that happen.

Chapter 20

End Days: Person *Not* on Hospice

Learn to light a candle in the darkest moments of someone's life.
Be the light that helps others see; it is what gives life its deepest significance.
~ *Roy T. Bennett,* The Light in the Heart

This time could be a nightmare or not, depending on the health of the person who is dying. If the person who is dying is simply aging, not having many health problems, naturally sleeping more, eating less, and losing energy, and the family is understanding of what is happening, the dying of the person could be very peaceful. It would be more supportive if the family would get on hospice service, but this type of person may not even be offered the opportunity if he or she is in a home setting. If the physician has not suggested hospice and the person has not been hospitalized for any reason, there will be no referral. It is quite likely the person either will die at home from heart failure, may die as 911 is called, or, in the days following, will be found unconscious.

But if the person who is approaching his or her dying has complicated health issues and/or unmanaged symptoms, his or her decline toward death could be very traumatic, especially if either the healthcare system or the family is refusing to address the fact that the person is actually dying. This is where most of the suffering at the end of life comes from: healthcare professionals are not taking the responsibility to tell the family the truth of their situation or are not realizing that the person is dying, or the family is not taking in the information and/or refusing to believe it. Usually it is a mixture of both.

If the family is fortunate enough to have a doula helping them in this type of scenario, they will be blessed indeed. You, as the doula, will look for opportunities to advocate for palliative care services for the family if they absolutely refuse hospice. They can and should still receive expert palliative care.

Make sure the person is physically comfortable (through expert palliative care), so the family's relational, spiritual, and emotional issues can be addressed. There is so much to do at the end of life. The end of life has its own "task list" for the time. The list may be longer or shorter, depending on how many legal, practical, relational, and personal tasks have been previously attended to.

Given that most people do not tend to the end-of-life task list (see "End-of-Life Task List" in the Supplemental Materials section) until right before death, you may be able to help with this. Find out as soon as you begin with a family. You may not have much time, for example, to sign such papers as the medical power of attorney if this hasn't already been done. You never know when the dying person will become unconscious.

If the person and the family refuse to talk with hospice and want to fight death until the end, support them in every way possible to accept what is happening now, whatever that is. Whatever is not acceptable, be part of finding the solution to make the situation acceptable. By having this mind-set, you will be encouraging peaceful solutions to what is going on now. People can have hope until their last breath. I have personally witnessed many people's having hope for cure as they went into an unresponsive state. It is not my place to take hope away but to accommodate their desires as they are alive. There are opinions that we should "break denial" and "make people see reality," but I personally do not believe in that unless the person who is dying is being harmed by decisions coming from that belief.

I will support people's doing anything they want, for the most part. I don't require that they accept that they are dying before I will serve them. It is not my place to be the person who makes them see they are dying. My role is to help bring peace to an often-frightening time and to walk alongside people with love and compassion. Yes, I have a lot of skill, and I can educate and guide, too. I can serve medically. I can do a lot besides love someone, but my default role is to love the person and the family. Everything else is secondary. It is not necessary to be medical to be an amazing doula. You serve them best if you take excellent care of yourself and are experienced in the ways of the dying, as you will be able to guide them through difficult experiences.

There are difficult experiences for the family as one of their beloved lies dying. When they don't allow hospice, they are really cutting off a huge network of support. So, if you know this is what you want to do as your vocation, become familiar with serving the dying; and the best way to do that is by serving your hospice either as a volunteer or in a role they have (physician, nurse, nurse assistant, social worker, chaplain, nurse practitioner). You need to see death and be part of a family that is facing someone's death to gain the experience you need for being really helpful to a family if you plan to do this as a community service.

If you are serving a family who has refused hospice and the person is dying, know that the person will most likely die in the hospital, or someone will call 911 if he or she should find the person unresponsive and already dead at home. Or the person may go in and out of the hospital several times, and there may be many highs and lows that are exhausting for all concerned. You can be helpful in getting them off that merry-go-round by suggesting palliative care.

Find out which hospital in your town has the best palliative care program (i.e., non-hospice palliative care), and find out which physicians in your town are great at managing the symptoms of various conditions. That way, if there is no freestanding palliative care clinic in your town (as is usually the case), you will have some options to give the family for assistance.

Key Point for "End Days" (person *not* on hospice service):
1. Know what hospital in your town has the best palliative-care program.
2. If there are no palliative certified physicians, know which physicians in your town are the best at certain symptoms. Call your local hospice and ask whom they might recommend.
3. Know that if the people you serve are going in and out of the hospital frequently, they most likely are not being managed well for their symptom control or their organ(s) may be failing. If their symptoms are not getting better, suggest a palliative-care consultation.
4. Do your best to help with practical concerns and help with last wishes. Even though the caregiver and family may not recognize that the person is dying, they still may want to participate in mending relationships, last trips, and so on.

Chapter 21

Pre-Death Vigil

You matter because you are you, and you matter to the end of your life.
We will do all we can not only to help you die peacefully, but also to live until you die.
~ Cicely Saunders

Whether or not you are working in hospice, if the person dies a natural death and takes time doing it, you may be present to assist in that person's pre-death vigil. This can be beautiful regardless of where the person is dying, as all are honoring their loved one's last moments on this earth.

The following is taken directly from my course, *Accompanying the Dying: A Practical Guide and Awareness Training.* These are some loving care suggestions:

1. Create a sacred space around the dying person. That includes what is spoken in front of the dying and decluttering and demedicalizing the space around the bed and room.
2. When you go to the bedside, identify yourself. Let the person know what you are going to do before you do it, or just let him or her know that you are there.
3. Keep the person fresh with daily bed baths with his or her favorite soap or fragrant oils or with spot washings of the face, head, underarms, and private area. Make sure his or her fingernails and toenails are cleaned and filed. I am surprised at how often a person has dirty fingernails. Please make sure they are clean.

4. Dress the person in his or her favorite bedclothes or comfortable clothing. If the family agrees, you can cut the clothing up the back with scissors to facilitate easy changing.

5. If the person's skin is cool and clammy, use warm rags with a favored fragrance to cleanse throughout the day. If he or she is warm from a fever, use a cool rag.

6. Make sure the family knows good mouth care. Use a Toothette® (stick with a sponge tip), moisten with a water and baking soda solution (1 tsp salt, 1 tsp baking soda to 1 qt water), and cleanse mouth by wiping the gum line, inner cheeks, and gums. Apply some artificial saliva if the person's mouth is dry, and lip balm to keep the lips moist. Use very gentle products to freshen his or her mouth. Maintain this throughout the day.

7. Make sure the family knows good eye care. At least once a day, use a warm rag to moisten the eye area and to thoroughly clean the skin around the eyes. Apply lubricating eye cream and artificial tears if the person's eyes appear dry. Maintain this throughout the day.

8. Most people love their head to be rubbed, their hair to be brushed, and their scalp to be massaged. Gently rub across the person's eyebrows and forehead. If the dying person likes this, do this regularly.

9. Keep encouraging family members to touch their dying loved one, but if it causes discomfort, keep them from doing so. (Some people don't believe in touching a dying person because they feel that it keeps the person on earth instead of letting him or her go.)

10. Use aromatic creams, oils, and lotions for generous foot/leg and hand/arm massages.

11. Take dirty briefs/pads to the outside trash immediately. Launder dirty sheets immediately so that smells do not become trapped in the room and/or the house.

12. Changing a person's position frequently will protect skin from breakdown. However, as a person nears imminent death, many people decide not to change positions so frequently. But there is another good reason to keep changing positions regularly—to help with the noisy congestion that can accumulate in the back of the throat. Changing positions will help with drainage. Put the head of the bed up and change the position side to side. Also, sometimes it helps if you are able to lower the head of the bed and raise the person's legs (if the person can tolerate it); that way, sometimes the drainage will go into his or her mouth, and you can get it out with a Toothette and then reposition the person into his or her favorite position.

13. Have a cool-mist humidifier to increase the humidity in the room. It will help with the dryness of the person's skin, mouth, eyes, and nose.

14. Don't ask questions of the dying. (He or she can't respond and can get agitated trying to answer questions.) Instead, tell stories. Encourage family members to tell the person how their day was, relate memories, and so on.

15. Check the person's skin. Make sure that the oxygen tubing isn't irritating the skin: check the nose, cheeks, ears, and jawline; you can pad the tubing to prevent skin irritation. Also make sure his or her ears are lying flat against the head on the side where the head is lying against the pillow. Make sure that the person's skin is not bunched up or being stretched on the side he or she is lying on, as well as on the rest of his or her body.

16. Have soft lighting in the room with the dying person. Use candles if you can. If you are in the hospital or somewhere where candles aren't allowed or wanted, use the artificial ones.

17. What are his or her favorite sounds? Music? Have these familiar sounds present. Harp music has been shown to be therapeutic with the dying. See if there is an organization in your city that will come play music as a part of palliative care (called Music Thanatology).

18. Put some of the person's favorite things (pictures, memorabilia, etc.) in view so they can be seen if the person should open his or her eyes.

19. Most people's feet are cold, so put warm socks on them. Cover the person with a favorite blanket.

20. Get a book of visualizations and/or meditations and read to the person. Or create them yourself for the dying person. Consider having some beautiful music playing in the background while you do.

21. Sit at the bedside with the dying, and if it's soothing to the person, hold his or her hand with thoughtful intention of a peaceful passing, prayers for his or her soul, and reassurance. Explain to family members that they can sit quietly and think loving thoughts toward their loved one. Encourage them to do it.

22. What are his or her favorite smells? Have a potpourri burner or essential oil burner in the room to maintain beautiful aromas.

Chapter 22

Death

Ever has it been that love knows not its own depth until the hour of separation.
~ Kahlil Gibran

The person has died. The physical transition of the body has happened. The person has taken his or her last breath; the pre-death vigil is over. Whether this is mostly a relief or a harder heartbreak depends on the person experiencing the death. Usually there is a tremendous release of emotion because the anticipated event has happened. Even though loved ones may feel that they are ready for the final moment, in my experience both personally and professionally, they are sometimes not fully ready. Dealing with the loss of their loved one is the beginning of a new road. Just like your walk with the family to this point, your loving support at this time will unfold as it needs to.

Some people will be in shock, even though they know it is happening. Some people will be very accepting as it is happening and just tremendously sad. Some will be very relieved that it is over, and this is the predominant feeling. Others will be devastated and very distraught in their grief. Of course, be prepared for anything, and let your intuition guide you.

Now there is the rest of the vigil. Many people want to stay longer with the body of their loved one than the typical two to four hours normally encouraged. Think about this and talk with your families about this before it happens. Would your family like some time with the body of their loved one? In the home-funeral industry, keeping the body three days or more is common.

Now, during this post-death vigil, we have time to integrate the transition from life to death and to move into the state of mourning. There is time to grieve with others and to transition into the new reality together.

The practicalities of a post-death vigil are significant and must be planned. For instance, if the family plans to keep the body for more than several hours, it must be kept on dry ice. The immediate family may be exhausted, need to be alone, and/or not want others present. Talk to your family and plan for what they want.

After someone has died, I encourage family members to stay with their loved one as long as they wish. I encourage them to wait before they call hospice and to have as much private time as they can now because once hospice is called, action begins to remove the body. They will never have this private time with their loved one again.

Often after the death, a time comes when people start wondering about what to do next. Remember to have the death plan and funeral plan completed beforehand so you can guide them during this time with activities they have already specified.

Offer to speak of peace and love and gratitude for the departed and of consolation for the family; invite them to participate. Ask if they would like to bathe the body and dress their loved one in a piece of favorite clothing. Maybe they don't want to participate but would like for you to do it. Usually at least one person will want to be a part of it, if the family wants the body bathed.

Remember to turn off the oxygen concentrator if it is on, and to get rid of as many hospital and medical-looking supplies and devices as possible after death. You've already done this to an extent during vigil, but you may have needed to keep some items out. Now is the time to get rid of all that is within eyesight.

If the family doesn't want to bathe the body fully, check the perineal area of the body and make sure it is clean and no stool or urine has been released. If needed, clean the area and take out the soiled briefs to the outside trash immediately and/or put the towels out to be laundered.

Views differ regarding touching the body after death. Some would say to encourage whoever would like to lie with the body, if he or she wants to, and give the person the privacy to do this. Some people want to but need "permission" to do so in the belief that others would think them odd if they do it. Let them know it is normal to want to be close to our loved one, especially because they will not be seeing them physically again.

Some faith traditions do not believe in touching the body after death or as a person is approaching death. Find out beforehand what the person's family believes in. If it is a matter of discomfort with a dead body rather than a belief in holding down the person's spirit, then help family members move past that discomfort. So many people have thanked me afterward for helping them touch their loved one's body.

Flow with what is going on and with what they want. They truly may not feel equipped to make any decisions, and in that case, you lead the way. When you are there, you will know how to proceed. Pray for guidance, trust what you hear, and follow your intuition.

If the person is on hospice, a hospice registered nurse will come out and pronounce the death. Know that you can tell the pronouncing nurse that your family wants to spend as much time with the body as possible. It is reasonable to say they may wait before calling hospice for an hour or so, but hospice usually wants to be told as soon as possible. It's just that once hospice is called, things usually move quickly in the direction of removing the body. If you want several hours with the body post-death, the best time to arrange this is before death. It is best to know the state laws about how much time is allowed before the body must be picked up. If the family has not had hospice care, the police will need to be called. They will send out officers to handle the death, and you will have to do things their way, of course.

If the family is doing a home funeral, then all this usually will have been arranged, but if the body is going to go to a funeral home or a crematory, then the family members need to prepare themselves for how much time they can spend with their loved one's body. Most people I have been with want to be with the body only two to four hours at home. But some have wanted it for several hours, and I made arrangements with the funeral home and sometimes had to call various ones who would accommodate the family for the length of time they wanted.

From death to the time of final disposition of the remains is a powerful time for the family and loved ones of the deceased. It takes time for the body and heart and mind to sync that the person we love so much has died. It takes time to shift into this new reality. That is why many post-death home vigil ceremonies last up to three days. It takes time to integrate the reality that someone has just died.

Take special care with the loved ones during the initial period post-death, at least for the first seven days or until the time of ceremony. Help them with practical matters and see how the primary caregiver would like to be supported during this time. So many are sleep-deprived and would be grateful for any help that would enable them to finally get some solid sleep. Some people will send the body for cremation and do not plan a ceremony for months after the death. There are so many possibilities. My main point post-death and for the initial week post-death is to support the primary caregiver and family especially during this time. This time is very tender as the new reality takes hold.

Chapter 23

Post-Death Vigil

Home funerals empower families and friends to begin the beautiful journey
of mending the tear in the fabric of their community that is rent apart
when someone they love dies.
~ Zenith Virago

The home funeral movement is sweeping the country and is profoundly empowering people. Home funerals are legal in every state and provide for the loving care for the deceased by the family from death until body disposition. Please go to the National Home Funeral Alliance website for all the information about this. It is beautiful and powerful.

A part of the home funeral is the post-death vigil. It is a sacred sitting with the deceased in the natural home environment. So many of us in this movement believe that taking more time with a loved one in processing the transition from life to death facilitates healthier grieving. It gives time for people to process the death and begin to integrate their new reality.

Some families prefer to be alone, and some open up this time for the community to visit and pay respects. In the United States, states vary on regulations regarding who can touch the body and how long you can keep a body at home. There are beautiful souls all over the world who will assist you with this and help you navigate through the laws of your state or country regarding disposition of remains.

Many who do post-death vigils or home funerals are prepared to keep the body for three days or longer. The National Home Funeral Alliance and the Funeral Consumer

Alliance are excellent resources regarding guidelines, laws, and people who are available to help.

YouTube has a beautiful home funeral video I recommend you see. It's called *Leon's Home Funeral*. Also, PBS has an incredible documentary titled *A Family Undertaking* (www.pbs.org/pov/afamilyundertaking). And there are many excellent trainings and workshops on how to do this and how to help others do it.

Chapter 24

Bereavement

Grief is not a feeling, it is a capacity.
It is not something that disables you, we are not on the receiving end of grief
we are on the practicing end of grief.
~ Stephen Jenkinson

Today, people are realizing and understanding the fact that processing the death and adjusting to the person's not being in their physical day-to-day life may take a lifetime. Wonderful information about living with loss acknowledges that this is not a six-month-to-a-year process and does not follow stages. Yes, the acute stage of dealing with the loss may be up to a year or so, but most people realize it may take a long time to integrate the loss in a way that feels comfortable. It may never.

If the family you are serving would like bereavement support, find out if the hospice they used has them. If they were not on hospice services, call one of your local hospices and ask if they have a program the community may use.

Not all hospices have a strong bereavement program. Many of them only send cards out at regular intervals. Get a list of resources from the hospice chaplain, social worker, or bereavement coordinator. If the hospice doesn't have a program more than cards, see if your town has another hospice with a strong bereavement program that includes counseling and that is available for people to attend who were not from their program.

These days we are fortunate also in that families can turn to several excellent bereavement-support groups on the internet. See "Bereavement Support" in the

Supplemental Materials section for some ideas. Your local hospice may have an excellent in-person or online support or know of some in your town. Ask them.

PART III

Things to Keep in Mind as an End-of-Life Doula

In the chapters that follow, I address several topics with which you should be familiar. No chapter is an intensive study on each topic (you can find several articles on the internet and books on each one). Rather, each chapter offers some food for thought as you develop your own opinions and boundaries on each issue. Really explore and develop your own relationship with each topic.

Chapter 25

Care of the Doula

If we do not know how to take care of ourselves and to love ourselves,
we cannot take care of the people we love.
Loving oneself is the foundation for loving another person.
~Thich Nhat Hanh

Yes, self-care is what I'm talking about. We know what it is; we know how to go about figuring out what works and what doesn't. We have to do it. If we don't, there is no way we can continue to be available to people in this way and stay genuine, flexible, intuitive, loving, gentle, strong, and in optimal physical health.

Most important, however, is that if you want to trust your intuition and discernment, you must take great care of yourself. If you do not, your fatigue will make you second-guess yourself. And if you do not take care of your own spiritual, emotional, and energetic needs well, you will project your needs onto the people you serve. Somehow, you will get emotionally "messy" with the people you want to help.

What takes the hit for you when you are not fully caring for yourself? What falls apart first? Second? Third? For me, my body is first. My body takes all the abuse of my self-neglect. Also, I can become emotionally needy. How are you when you are not caring for yourself? What do people say to you, about you? Are you told you are rigid? A victim? A martyr? Do you get sick frequently? Are you prone to accidents? Do you get depressed and unable to function? What is your response to lack of self-care? How do you fall apart? Of course, I don't want you to fall apart, burn out, or get sick, but all of that will happen if you don't take meticulous care of yourself as you do this work.

I make self-care a part of my daily plan. It is a necessary component of my day. I schedule in my spiritual time, the things that make me feel good, time to prepare healthy food, go to the grocery store, do my walks, feel the fresh air, rest, do my rituals, have my feel-good moments, take pauses, and meditate. I love to put my crystals in the moonlight after a good wash. I love the sound of my Tibetan bowl. I love to read my Jesus prayer book, the Bible, and other spiritual readings. I love to read the writings of women who take deliberate, loving care of themselves and know their worth. I love to meditate and journal. I love to read the writings of philosophers and poets. All those activities feed my soul.

I make time to systematically support myself spiritually and emotionally. I plan it in to my day; I plan it into my cooking, my shopping, and my garden when I have one. I create self-care habits that nourish me. I look for more ways to do this, and I love listening to how others do it.

It is not a luxury; it is focused and loving care that I want to give myself because I know how much energy it can take to be available the way I am. I'm gratefully expectant of receiving an abundance of love and nourishment from my Spiritual Source. Make it an absolute joyride. If you already do, good for you!

For those of you who are thinking I'm making too much of it, please give yourself a month of adding something very special to your self-care routine. If you don't have such a routine presently, please give yourself a month of doing something, just one thing, on purpose, with intention that will nurture your mind, body, soul, heart, spirit, consciousness, and senses in some way. Journal this month as you implement this. See if you feel or think differently at the end of thirty days.

If you are somewhere in the middle, where you value self-loving care but don't have the time or just can't seem to create space for it or it, just doesn't seem important enough for some reason, then commit to implementing a daily love offering and make sure that no matter what, you will do one type of intentional self-care per day. Please journal for at least a few weeks as you bring this back into your life.

Chapter 26

Dying "Organically"

Death never takes a wise man by surprise; he is always ready to go.
~ Jean de la Fontaine

To begin this chapter, I would like to address a few angles of the definition of the word *organic*.

As we die, our organs shut down one by one, or sometimes all at once or in a combination. The medical definition of *organic* is *of or pertaining to organs*, but that is not what I'm referring to here. Nor am I referring to the fact that our bodies contain a lot of carbon. *Organic* also refers to something developing as a matter of natural progression; in farming and food production, it refers to not using artificial chemicals and pesticides in creation and processing.

In the realm of dying, and for the purposes of this book, I define dying organically as letting nature take its course, or supporting ourselves well, as our body is completing its natural cycle and usefulness or creating an atmosphere of peace and healing as our bodies are dying on this earth. Or, stated in the negative, it is not fighting to live while the body is dying, with artificial means via medications, equipment, surgeries, processes, and other invasive means.

Dying organically means allowing our bodies to unwind in the natural progression toward death when we are dying. It means supporting our bodies in this process so that we can tend to the very important emotional, psychological, and spiritual work of our dying self. This is what is so hard for us. Thank you, Dr. Michael Barbato, for reminding me of this. He, of course, in his beautiful humility, cites the work of Stephen Levine that explains more about this, in his book *Who Dies?* Please make reading this book a priority for getting a handle on why we fight death so hard.

Look at dying a natural death as you would look at growing something organically. You want to support the natural process. You are not doing anything to hasten it or prolong it. You are not adding weird chemicals, anything that would grossly alter the process. You want to keep with the natural rhythms of life, the day and the night.

Dying an organic death is letting things come as they do and not fighting it with artificial means that could actually hurt us more than it will help. It is letting things unfold as they will. There are medications and natural remedies that can help the body unwind and die peacefully. The body sometimes has difficulty dying if one or more organs are severely compromised or damaged from an illness or treatments for that illness.

There is a strong push right now in some circles for little medicinal support as someone is dying. I don't understand this push. Some people's bodies are severely damaged from the treatments used to try to survive. Their bodies have been severely compromised by artificial processes that can-do extreme damage in the attempt to save someone's life. Also, sometimes a person just needs a little medicine to help the body let go and help the whole system wind down peacefully.

Each organ, as it shuts down, affects every other body system, and sometimes this process is not easy. We have what we need in the United States to manage dying well medicinally. What is lacking is the holistic support of the person and family. The biggest support to an organic death is spiritual, emotional, and energetic. Know what is important to the person. Do it.

Accepting that our body is failing and will not recover will prevent days, weeks, and months of needless suffering because we will not be adding in surgeries and treatments and drugs that may do little more than add time and possibly a lot of harm. Not all time bought by high-tech interventions will add suffering-free time; sometimes they actually add more time spent suffering.

Allowing natural death is not the same thing as refusing treatment that would save your life. Whatever your opinion is about euthanasia, allowing natural death is not that. It is not committing suicide to refuse to attempt to save a dying body that is dying from an irreversible illness.

One day we each will die, regardless of what we do to stop it. To be ill and to be dying from that illness are not failures. It is our ending on this planet. That is all. There is no judgment to it.

Chapter 27

It's About Love

How can the dead be truly dead when they still live
in the souls of those who are left behind?
~ Carson McCullers, The Heart is a Lonely Hunter

Please welcome the end-of-life doula, midwife, home funeral guide, celebrant, and other types of beautiful roles and services in the "death empowerment" movement over the last twenty years or so. There are many names for those souls who want to bring peace to the end of life.

We are *not* part of a medical movement; our movement is of the heart. And it is a movement about human decency. It is no surprise that we have not been supporting ourselves to die well in these last decades as we have created tremendous medical miracles of life at all costs.

Many people today and over the years have committed their lives to helping people avoid dying a miserable death because of the medical miracles we have gained. There have always been people all along the way, alongside the medical miracles, who tried to remind us of our humanity and of the ethics of what we were getting ourselves into; but for the most part, their voices were too quiet to be heard above the manic search for the cure and for everlasting life.

Caring and loving others is programmed into our DNA. It is in our ancient wisdom and our heritage to accompany our sick and dying. We have forgotten this during the past several decades, as we have been mostly fighting death instead. So instead of loving the person as they die, many of us have been anxiously terrified as we watch and have been a part of fighting death. No one is single-handedly to blame here, but collectively perhaps we moved too fast with technology—at such a fast clip that most of us were all caught up in it, we suffered greatly for it, and we saw our loved ones suffer. We know better now.

So, the death positive or death empowerment movement going on now is, at its core, about love. It's about loving care for one another and loving support for one another as we die. It is about supporting our bodies, emotions, minds, spirits, and souls. It is about acknowledging the reality of the life cycle. It is about acknowledging that people die at every age and that it will always be like this. It is about loving people enough to be present and not try to fix their emotional and spiritual suffering; it is about being a companion as each of us works out our own dying. It is about witnessing, caring, and standing by. It is about *love*.

No matter what else you do as you serve the dying, love them. Love yourself first. Build your world in self-love and compassion so that you may genuinely be gifting that to the people you serve.

They will not remember so much what you did as how you made them feel. Remember that and love them.

People feel you more than they listen to you. Love them.

Love and compassion present and abundantly flowing from you, out of you, is your greatest strength.

This is your daily chore, your biggest task on your to-do list: *Love yourself* so that you may love the people you serve with genuine and authentic concern and support.

Chapter 28

Fighting Death

Let yourself be open and life will be easier.
A spoon of salt in a glass of water makes the water undrinkable.
A spoon of salt in a lake is almost unnoticed.
~ Buddha Siddhartha Gautama Shakyamuni

We can all agree that we have created mind-blowing ways to stay alive despite the odds. We have seen the miracles and the horrors in our lives, our parents' lives, our grandparents' lives, and our great-grandparents lives. We have marveled at how we can live far past our "expiration date."

Sometimes the benefit is simply life for life's sake, and that is enough. Sometimes people actually feel like they have quality in their lives despite their new severe limitations, and sometimes people have second chances at near or full capacity or better than their previous lives.

And now we are coming into claiming our right to die a natural or organic death as well. Can you imagine that we have come to a place in our history where people sometimes feel ashamed when they refuse the high-tech options of fighting death?

We are claiming our right to a natural death *without* feeling the shame of "giving up the fight." We have swung so far in the direction of "life at all costs" that what has come with it is tremendous pressure for people to choose "artificial" life-sustaining treatments when they actually did not want to. There was pressure from family, from the medical establishment, and from themselves. For the people who want this, fantastic! You have it. By default, you will receive this treatment. If you do not, you must have Advance Directives. (See "Advance Directives" in the Supplemental Materials section.)

Note that I am not referring to hastening our death; I am not referring to euthanasia. What I am referring to is choosing to allow natural death. Many of us want to quit fighting the natural progression of death. When we do quit fighting it, we will actually die a quieter, more peaceful death.

So much suffering comes with fighting death. So many of the treatments and procedures and processes that people go through to extend their lives actually create tremendous suffering. This is the "rest of the story" most people do not receive when they are making major decisions about treatments and surgeries that will affect the rest of their lives.

Physicians, nurses, and medical personnel know this. It grieves them, too, that they do not have the time to adequately explain the advantages of the treatments they offer, much less share with you all the disadvantages. The other side (the cons) to every treatment offered is real and can actually create tremendous physical suffering.

You will hear many people say, "Just unhook me if I get like that." I ask you, "*Like what*?" I have taken care of many people who, because of their treatment choices, have lived miserable lives with tubes out of every orifice to handle every need. But tubes fall out, their mechanics promote erosion of the skin around the tube, skin decays, and body fluids sting terribly. And this is just the beginning of what actually happens to people.

Getting "the rest of the story" is my way of asking you to ask for the whole story. Ask for the top three most negative things that could happen with each treatment you are being advised to get. Many people are told that the alternative to the treatment is death. By the time I took care of people as a hospice nurse, many people told me that they would have preferred death to what they chose to endure in trying to beat the odds. Many said they felt left in the dark and had no idea what to do except to accept what was offered. Ask for projected timelines. By how long may this treatment extend your life? What will you be dealing with potentially if you survive? What will it be like if you refuse the treatment? In the days that remain, how will the suffering, if any, look as opposed to what the results of the surgery or treatment looks like if it doesn't go well?

For many people, trying every treatment will always be their choice; they will always choose anything to live rather than the possibility of death without it. That is a noble choice. So is not risking negative consequences and risking the possibility of earlier death. That is a noble choice as well.

We are fully supported in our present system to choose to fight death. If you choose instead not to fight death, count on this book as support. This book supports bringing peace to people as they face their dying. If you choose to fight or if you choose to not fight, I support you.

Some of the people in your life may fight death until they have no more energy to fight. There are some situations, such as that of the young, accidents, sudden aggressive illness, or whatever reason, in which people will fight like hell to live.

Don't judge people's resistance to death just because you may feel it is okay to die, regardless of your age. Some people feel that death is fair at any age, and that not all of us will live to a ripe old age. Some people wish they would die now; they feel too old and broken down to continue living. Some people's hearts are so broken that they no longer want to live, yet they are still here, even though they will themselves to die every day. So, as you walk with people through dying, you will witness many things.

There are many scenarios regarding how "fighting death" may look in someone you know. As a doula, the best thing to do is to lovingly listen to the people you are serving without judgment. Listen to what they want and be a part of helping them have that.

Chapter 29

Denial

Don't believe everything you think.
~ Byron Katie

I almost didn't call this chapter "denial" because I don't feel the word is the best one when describing someone's coping with the reality they are dying or that a loved one is dying. It is useful here so here we go.

Regarding the Primary Caregiver. Please don't be a part of a "we need to break their denial" campaign. Unless the primary caregiver is the one making decisions for the dying and the primary caregiver is making a decision that will hurt the dying person or is against their wishes, I am not sure it is necessary to break the caregiver's denial.

I don't even like the phrase "breaking the denial."

What is happening is that the people involved are trying to cope with the fact that a person they love with all their heart is dying and will no longer be here. They each have a long history with this person and there may be many shared traumas or beautiful moments that are so painful to integrate right now that they are doing everything they can to cope. We have no idea of the mental, psychological, emotional, or spiritual state of the person who is coping and should not feel like we do. Unless you are a trained mental healthcare worker (chaplain, social worker, therapist, shaman, etc.), leave denial assessments alone.

Regarding the Dying Person. You will hear many people in the hospice profession state that a person always knows truly when he or she is dying. I used to believe that, but not anymore. I have spent time at the bedside of hundreds of people, and I would agree that many people do know they are dying. But more than a few really don't know.

We never know what is in the heart and mind of anyone. All we have to go on is what someone says to us and how he or she behaves. We take what people tell us at face value sometimes, and sometimes we are very busy reading between all the lines. Good luck with that. Get out of the judging of this. If the person looks like he or she is dying but says he or she is not dying and is, in fact, planning a trip to Cuba, I would help them plan that trip if asked.

Let loving and advocating for the dying person be your guide and primary concern, and let loving the primary caregiver by deep listening be a close second.

Accept in yourself your judgment about the people involved fighting their death or fighting the acceptance of their death or being in denial. Do you have feelings about it when it is happening? If you are triggered by this, why? Understanding is more important than "getting them out of denial." As a doula, any situation you are in that makes you feel emotionally charged should be looked at by you as your own issue that needs to be addressed so you can be a better servant.

The less you are emotionally triggered by situations, the clearer you will be and the better able you will be to serve at the highest level. You must do your own self-care, which involves continually bringing your emotional and spiritual issues into awareness for addressing.

Chapter 30

The Hospital Is No Place to Die

Seven in ten Americans (71 percent) prefer to die at home, if possible.
~ Kaiser Family Foundation Study

The hospital is no place to die (for most). Maybe for most people this is true, and this is what everyone writing about the perfect death is saying, isn't it? Just know there are some people whose preference would be to die in the hospital. They feel safer there, and some do find comfort in hospitals.

Overall, the hospital is probably not the best place for most people to die. And sometimes it may be the best place for some people to die. Let go of absolute judgments about it and focus on the person you are serving and what he or she wants. Help the person make that happen.

In 2005, when my mother died, I knew I wanted to be part of bringing death home and out of hospitals. I also knew, long before hospice was even thought of, about a lot of things that would relieve suffering (palliative medicine, the medicine hospice uses). I didn't know anyone was working on this grassroots movement of bringing "the relief of suffering" (palliative care) to people long before hospice was considered. It is true that palliative medicine is appropriate for people from day 1 of diagnosis with a serious illness; it is *not* just for the dying.

I had been working in hospice five years and had never heard anyone talk about that. I just saw every day that so much suffering was happening in the world before hospice, and it did not need to be. We had answers in hospice that were simple and were known. Why were people not using them before they began hospice care? I did not understand this. What should have been happening was not. Many people were dying before they even got to hospice, and they were suffering terribly. This is still happening. It's 2018, and this is unconscionable.

If a person must die in the hospital, then it makes sense that every hospital would have excellent palliative care and especially excellent palliative care for the dying. Hospice service should not be the only way to die well. If you are serving a family whose relative is in the hospital, and that person is dying and not dying well, ask for hospice to come and get the person comfortable. Most hospices will come to the hospital and take care of him or her. Even if the person is dying well in the hospital, hospice provides excellent emotional and spiritual support and will come to the hospital to walk with a person through the death.

Chapter 31

Learning to Die

Wisdom comes with the ability to be still. Just look and just listen. No more is needed.
Being still, looking, and listening activates the non-conceptual intelligence within you.
Let stillness direct your words and actions.
~ Eckhart Tolle, Stillness Speaks

Here is a thought: What if dying isn't all about just the person who is dying? What if the task facing the person who is dying is to show the people around him or her how to die? Let's just go with this a minute.

If it is true that we are on this planet to love and serve each other through life, and we are each other's teachers, then this doesn't stop when we face our death.

What do we want to teach the people closest to us? Do we need to focus on anyone but ourselves when it is our time to die? Isn't this all about us? Shouldn't everyone drop everything and focus squarely on us and our needs? Yes? No?

In the death-positive movement, we talk of death as being a community event, and we want to bring dying back into the fold of the family and the community and out of the isolation of lonely hospital rooms. If death is really a community event, then our dying is informing not only our own life but also the lives of the people around us.

When it is time for each of us to die, it will be new for us, and maybe we will be frightened. Or maybe we won't. We will be dealing with it however we will, gracefully or not. And all eyes are on us, like it or not. Everyone around us will be gaining insight into dying and death through our experience with it.

Not only will we be learning to die ourselves, but we will be teaching others about dying. More important, however, we will be sharing who we are and how we want to be cared for during this time. We will be reviewing our own end-of-life task list and checking off our last to-do items.

In the death empowerment movement, what most people are advocating for is giving our own death the acknowledgment and knowing its certainty, planning for its inevitability, and making our choices known and being responsible for ourselves and the planet in that planning. Also, it is sharing the wisdom in the process and leaving a legacy of love and healing for our survivors. That's all. Simple, right?

Chapter 32

Antibiotics Use

Most people do not listen with the intent to understand.
Most people listen with the intent to reply.
~ Stephen Covey

When we are healthy or expected to live for quite a while, antibiotics are often suggested and used, and most people do not think twice about it. There is a movement against the use of antibiotics for most situations, but that is not what I'm referring to in this discussion.

Here is what I want to bring to your attention: Just because someone near death has an infection, it will not always be appropriate, necessary, or advisable to give antibiotics for it. There are ways to handle pain, if there is any. The antibiotic is given to cure or treat an infection, not to cure pain. While it is true that an infection may cause pain, as in the case of an ear infection, a bladder infection, and the like, an infection does not always cause pain. Even a bladder infection, especially in the elderly, does not always cause pain.

Don't be alarmed if the experienced palliative physician or nurse does not recommend antibiotics for a dying person if he or she happens to be diagnosed with an infection or are even dying from that infection. The side effects of the antibiotics may cause more harm than anything the infection could possibly cause.

Discuss the pros and cons with your family. Know that it is common in end-of-life situations to not treat infections with antibiotics but to do whatever is necessary to keep the person comfortable.

Chapter 33

Feeding Tube

He who asks question remains a fool for five minutes.
He who does not ask remains a fool forever.
~ Chinese Proverb

This section is not to argue for or against the use of a feeding tube but to give you food for thought.

1. A person can aspirate (choke) from the contents of a feeding tube just as easily (some say more so), as a person who has difficulty swallowing. Do not be misled into a false sense of security that a person will not aspirate with a feeding tube.
2. Just because you can give several cans of calorie-dense fluid into a tube doesn't mean you should. Lab tests show that a dying person does not process the calories that are being forced inside anyway. So, what good is it doing?
3. Notice also whether they are having diarrhea. Does the diarrhea reduce when the amount of fluid you put in the tube is decreased?
4. Diarrhea from fluids that are not processing through the body well but instead are pooling in the tissue will exacerbate skin breakdown and terrible bedsores come from them. Bedsores (decubitus ulcers) can be very painful.
5. Is the person's bottom raw from diarrhea? (Again, be extremely aware of skin breakdown.)

6. Does the skin feel "mushy"? Do you feel the fluid retaining in the tissues? Again, this is a warning sign of trouble ahead for someone whose circulation may be slowing down and who may not be eliminating their wastes appropriately.
7. Does the person vomit or regurgitate often? This is another sign of intolerance of the feeding.
8. Know that fluids accumulate in body organs and skin (the largest body organ) and tissue when the circulation is slowing down (lungs included). This may make it harder for someone to breathe.
9. Basically, read about fluid overload in a dying person and see if your loved one is experiencing any of these symptoms.

Let some of these answers guide your family on whether now is the time to be using artificial nutrition. They may be using the tube just for medications. Talk to the hospice, a palliative physician, or a nurse for the best way to administer the medications that the dying person needs right now.

Chapter 34

Mechanical Ventilation

Better to get hurt by the truth than comforted with a lie.
~ Khaled Hosseini

If the person who is dying is not on hospice, there may be a chance that he or she will be put on a ventilator at some point in the process of their decline if they are unable to breathe independently. When a person is dying, when the underlying disease process will not improve, putting someone on this only prolongs his or her death. It keeps him or her oxygenated until the lungs or another body part (or parts) fail. It will definitely buy time if that is what is wanted. But then the issue of getting off the ventilator can be very emotional and guilt laden.

Every person who dies a natural death will stop breathing. That is part of the process. Putting the person on a ventilator doesn't add to his or her quality of life. Medications can be easily used to help with breathing as we are dying.

People tend to say things like "unplug" the person or "we pulled the plug" and so on, to refer to taking someone off mechanical ventilation. This adds a burden of guilt and a feeling of "playing God" that is so painful to a family. The option should not be offered to a person with advanced illness who is dying. That is irresponsible in most cases. Who says it is "playing God" to put them on that when we know the person is dying? Are we fighting God? It can be argued either way.

The point here is that the ventilator is an inappropriate treatment for a dying person, one that adds unnecessary fear and guilt for families. They have enough to deal with in losing their loved one. That pain is enough.

Hospice deals with people daily whose lungs are failing them and can deal humanely with this issue. You may always ask the family if they would like to speak with hospice (a doctor must order this consultation) and get their assessment of the situation to continue this treatment if started. It is an emergent situation that would make the hospital doctors choose this intervention to begin with. If a person is at the end of life, it is wise to bring in experts about end-of-life symptom management and hospice is the expert in end-of-life situations. Hospitals ask for them to come and evaluate patients all the time and respect the consultation they receive.

Chapter 35

Euthanasia and Physician-Assisted Death

*We can never judge the lives of others, because each person
knows only their own pain and renunciation.*
~ Paulo Coelho

As a doula in community service, you will decide what kinds of people to focus on. Will you serve all people, or will you specialize in infant death or children or people with dementia and so on? I have heard some discuss whether they would support a person who chooses physician-assisted death.

This is an emotionally complicated situation, and if you decide you want to support others through this, I would highly recommend you take the training of Compassion and Choices or of another group that specializes in the issues surrounding physician-assisted death.

Just like abortion and capital punishment, this topic is loaded and polarizing. If you are going to support families through this, know all sides of the issue well. If you are not going to support people who want this, have a gentle way of saying you are not available for it.

We are compassionate in all matters with people. This is a very tender topic, and our role as doulas here is not so much to sway opinion; it is to facilitate discussion. This topic has brought more people into discussion about death and dying in the United States than has Death Café. You have the potential to bring more healing and awareness to your community by facilitating discussion of heated topics than by choosing sides and focusing on yourself and *your* side. We are here as channels of peace, as guides, for the most part. But then again, perhaps your vision and mission *are* a single-issue platform. That is wonderful too.

Just be mindful about your path and what kind of support you want to provide. What is your main mission? How would you best support that? Just be willing to take the consequences of any decision you make for yourself in your practice.

If you are a doula in private practice in your community, unless you want to be the mouthpiece for this particular movement (on either side), I would recommend being discreet on the topic in public. It may hijack your practice if you are not. It is a serious topic worthy of serious discussion and respect. Do you want to be identified with this or any other single issue that is polarizing to people?

Chapter 36

Terminal Sedation

*True compassion means not only feeling another's pain but also
being moved to help relieve it.*
~ Daniel Goleman

This sounds a little scary to people who have not heard the phrase before. *Terminal sedation* is when the medical team and the family make the decision to give medications to relieve tremendous suffering, knowing that the effects of the medication may hasten death. It is not the same thing as physician-assisted death.

Physician-assisted death is when medication is given knowingly to end the life of the person. That is the whole point.

In terminal sedation, the point is to relieve the suffering related to a particular symptom. The dose of the medication may need to become so large that it may kill the person. Just like in surgery or any other medical treatment, one of the dangers is that you may die. In terminal sedation, this is what is happening: the dose that will be necessary to relieve the suffering of a particular symptom may cause death. It may not, but it may.

Some people feel it is merely semantics, but we can clearly see it is not. One treatment is *meant* to kill a person, and the other treatment is meant to *relieve* a symptom but *may* kill the person more quickly than if the disease progresses naturally.

PART IV

Do I Want to Serve My Community as an End-of-Life Doula?

Just because you have a heartfelt interest in serving the dying or facilitating conversation around empowering others to die well, it doesn't mean you want to have a full-time or even a part-time practice doing it.

But some of you do want to do this and be an active part of supporting your community. There is nothing you'd rather do than be a part of bringing peace to others at the end-of-life. Some of you may need a little help deciphering your feelings.

Here is my attempt to help you sort through this. A private practice is not for everyone. Starting a nonprofit is not for everyone, either. You will see for yourself over time how you want to manifest this gift and this calling you have. We do need you.

Some of the ways to serve:
- ➢ Part-time practice
- ➢ Menu item of a current full-time holistic practice
- ➢ Full-time practice solely as an end-of-life doula
- ➢ Community educator and facilitator of discussion
- ➢ Patient advocacy specializing in advanced illness issues
- ➢ Volunteer program within hospice or other community organization
- ➢ Create a collective of end-of-life doulas

Chapter 37

Assess Your Commitment

If your goals aren't synced with the substance of your heart,
then achieving them won't matter much.
~ Danielle LaPorte

An assessment tool I developed, the End-of-Life Doula Commitment Tool, may help you think this through. You may be the go-to person in your circle of family and friends whether every time someone gets seriously ill or is dying, you seem to be the one that people call on. Or you have a rich background in the end-of-life field and are trying to figure out you want to delve deeper into helping others and how you would do it.

You are trying to answer the question, "Is this work really for me?" You may know you are drawn to the subject matter and that your heart yearns to serve people, but you are trying to discern how committed you are to this type of service. So answer the following questions. Do not think too much—go with your gut. I have developed the EOL Doula Commitment Tool to help you assess your level and type of commitment to this type of work.

End-of-Life Doula Commitment Tool

Directions. Rate each of the ten statements that follow as
   5 – *Absolutely Yes!*
   4 – Yes
   3 – Maybe/I Don't Know

2 – No

1 – *Definitely No!*

1. I am (mostly) confident that I can do this work and do it well. I know what I need to step out on my own in my community.
2. I am certain that I am supposed to serve others with my "calling."
3. I would be able to better care for myself if I were serving my community as an end-of-life doula—it would fit my lifestyle better.
4. Pick one of the following statements and rate it.
    a. Even though I am *not* a medical professional, I have a special gift(s) that will bless a person on his or her journey and/or the person's family.
    b. I am a medical professional and know that I want to serve in a broader role than I am able to serve within my present organizational role.
5. I would be more authentically "me" if I were serving my community as an end-of-life doula.
6. I am 100 percent committed to serving the dying and their families in my community.
7. If I could support myself doing this work, I would give my two-weeks' notice and begin today.
8. I am comfortable being a pioneer in a new field, a trailblazer among trailblazers.
9. I am comfortable with marketing my services.
10. I know exactly how I want to integrate my experiences, education, and spiritual/emotional gifts.

Scoring: Determine the type of commitment you want to make to this, based on how you answered the questions. Really pay attention to your inner voice.

If you scored 35 to 50, you know you are pretty determined to make it through the rough spots, self-doubts, and obstacles that may come your way.

If your score is 20 to 34, search deep inside to see what part of all this appeals to you, and focus on that part.

If you score to 10 to 19, maybe it's just a passing curiosity, and that is okay, too. Or maybe it means you will be happiest being the go-to person for your family and friends and are really not interested in serving as an independent practitioner in your community.

What was your score? Are you leaning toward building a practice?

Whether you want a private practice or not, if you truly desire to explore your passion for serving the dying, I am honored and most grateful to accompany you as you explore in my sacred space for mentoring, our School of Accompanying the dying. Learn more at www.school.accompanyingthedying.com. We have a powerful program of self-transformation as you learn everything you need to serve others well. People have been coming to me for years to learn the art-of-the-doula way—not something you can learn in a weekend workshop for sure, mine or anyone else's.

Learning the art of the doula way is something that takes time and patience. Jumping through testing hoops does not make you better at it. Devoting yourself to study and self-care, gaining experience, and committing to a community is the true path of the end-of-life doula. Establish this first. *Then*, if you want to develop a private practice do so. I don't recommend doing it all at the same time.

Learn the end-of-life doula issues and all that goes into serving people at this time. Learn about yourself along the way. As you do this, you will see exactly where you fit in and what you want to create.

Blessings on your journey, and I hope to meet you on this beautiful path.

Chapter 38

Considerations Prior to Building a Private Practice

I've learned that people will forget what you said,
people will forget what you did,
but people will never forget how you made them feel.
~ Maya Angelou

Hopefully the assessment tool in Chapter 37 helped give you more clarity and validation of what is in your heart. If you are leaning heavily toward building a private practice, then consider the following before you dive in.

There are five major things to think about before building a practice:

1. *Don't quit your day job!* I'm not going against the "law of attraction" or any positive thinking mantras by telling you this reality: We are not on most people's radar yet. They do not know we are here. Most people are aware they are frustrated, frightened, anxious, overwhelmed, and grieved, but they have no idea there is an emerging group of people in a "new" role that can help them. It is changing, though. I'm sure you can feel that. You are much closer to supporting yourself in 2018 than I was in 2005. I would still have a plan to segue into this full time if you are counting on your present monthly income.

   I am doing all I can to bring awareness to this movement as are many others. At Quality of Life Care, I have created many public education initiatives like our podcast, *Journey with Deanna*, and our blog. Our podcast began as the world's first palliative care radio podcast, *The Journey Radio*. I have a free Learning Center on our Facebook Page for all aspiring doulas to learn as much as they can. There are other lovely people who have, in the last several years, come on to the scene who are teaching all aspects of end-of-life care and its wonderful! We are in the second stages of a burgeoning movement—hold on! *And* I want you to develop a beautiful practice based on your heart and not fear (fear of making ends meet). So even though our economy would support your full-time practice right now (personal-companion companies are a billion-dollar business), you need to be prepared to pay your bills on a monthly basis until this practice can support you.

2. *You must know what you are doing when you are dealing with a person who is dying and his or her family.* Just because you have the desire to serve and have a heart full of compassion doesn't mean you know how to talk to a person who is dying or how to be supportive of a family at this time.

   Trust what you don't know and strengthen yourself there. One step at a time, continue to develop. I honor and respect your research into doing this sacred work. It means you respect the people you want to serve. There is no international or national accreditation governing board to oversee end-of-life companions and guides, so you must be driven by this value yourself. We are a self-regulating field, and so you must know your own limits and practice with impeccable standards.

3. *Lead with your heart.* Nobody cares what your credentials are when they are amid overwhelming grief. They want to know you are there and that you care. They need to feel you in the room. They don't need your head knowledge or your philosophy of the cultural aspects of death since 1293. They need *you!*

   Presence is the foundation, the cornerstone, of our practice. To be present emotionally and spiritually for someone and his or her family, you yourself must be grounded, aware, conscious, and mindful. Presence is a must. This is the basis for all your work, no matter what else you may offer a family.

4. *Let people know you are here.* I encourage you to create your awareness campaigns (i.e., marketing efforts) in ways that are true to your own values, which for most are education, inspiration, and empowerment. There are other ways to become known in your community as the go-to person, like creating a book or movie discussion group. You must be willing to step into the shoes of the trailblazer, as there are few paths outside of hospice for us. Most people run from death, whereas you are running toward it. You are truly unique and *must* have the calling to behave in such a way! I cannot wait to meet you.

5. *Engage in radical self-care for the long haul.* Whatever your faith tradition, you must be prepared to amp it up when you come into this field. You come face to face with some of the hardest emotions, situations, and times people will ever face. Yes, we know this can be beautiful. That is why you want to do this, and yes, some people will ask for you because they want to create sacred space and a beautiful dying experience, *and* many people won't be in this head and heart space.

To do this work well, you must be respectful of your heart, and of the realities of being between two worlds often, and of being in the presence of significant grief. You can be in this space if you are taking care of yourself in a loving and consistent way, and you are somehow spiritually supporting yourself on a deep level. These two things, self-care and spiritual support, must happen because you not only need them to be able to do this work over the long haul but also need them to be able to stay in the present moment with the person you are with and not drift off yourself.

I need to be very blunt right now. To have a private practice is hard work. You are self-employed if you choose this; you are responsible for every aspect of your practice. There is the service side, which we all love, and there are two other sides (think of a three-legged stool). You must market or promote your services and you must maintain the business—pay your bills as well as do all the administrative tasks. This can be all-consuming until you are able to hire help or assemble one heck of a volunteer team. It is not for everyone, as the hours can be grueling and always remember that everything you say yes to you are saying no to something or someone else.

PART V

Supplemental Materials

In this section I offer you additional food for thought, checklists, and resources to help you help others. My hope is you will find it empowering, as it will deepen your understanding of what you should know and what you can do to strengthen yourself in the role as one who accompanies another through dying.

I. The Second Wave and My Story

The first wave of alternative death work was the hospice movement, which began with Dame Cecily Saunders in the late 1960s. We have seen what has occurred in the world relating to dying in peace and dignity since hospice came on the scene then. Hospice was an alternative movement from modern-day healthcare at the time and was brought into mainstream healthcare around the world.

Moving strongly since about 2000 or so is what I call the second wave. We are having the conversations about dying, about advance directives, about funeral choices. Surveys say we want to die at home. We have hit the roof with living at all costs and are deciding it isn't for us. We are saying we want to care for own dying. Because it has been so long since most of us have taken care of our dying, we need to be shown how.

"Practitioners" in this second wave have been involved in the hospice movement directly over the years or have wanted to be of service but have not seen exactly how they fit in outside of a volunteer role with hospice or the hospital system. Many of them have been volunteers, but they want to do more. They want to make this their life's work, and they need to make a living. They have ideas of what may serve people at this time. They have ideas for services, programs, and initiatives, and they want to spearhead them. They are not satisfied just helping now and then after a long workweek or with having strict organizational boundaries.

So, as all of this has been happening, customers' dissatisfaction with the funeral industry was growing. They didn't want to pay exorbitant prices for a funeral, and they wanted choices. In 1978 the Funeral Consumer Alliance formed to assist in consumers' interests. Cremation gained popularity in the 1970s. Leadership in bringing death care home was beginning to take place through such people as Jessica Mitford, Ernest Morgan, William Wendt, Lisa Carlson, Nancy Poer, and Tamara Slayton, among others.

In the 1990s, home-funeral trainings were beginning to take off around the United States through Natural Transitions and Final Passages. In the mid-2000s, when I decided to become a death midwife (I thought I had made it up), I had no idea all this was going on. I stumbled into a home-funeral workshop in 2007 in Austin at a Funeral Consumer Alliance Conference, and I've never been the same since. I noticed then that people who helped with home funerals, more often than not, called themselves death midwives. I didn't want to confuse what was happening in the eyes of anyone paying attention, so I called myself an end-of-life doula because I had no interest in assisting with home funerals at the time. I felt that this was a new movement, one that would eventually become quite strong, and I did not want to muddy the waters. It felt like the right thing to do.

In the 2000s, there was little talk about people serving outside of hospice. Shira Ruskay Center in New York City had an end-of-life doula program for training volunteers to serve via weekly visits to individuals who were alone. The program now is called Doula Program to Accompany and Support. I spoke with people in the program at the time, and it wasn't appropriate for me to train with them. I realized that I didn't need to. I knew how to deal with families at the end of life in a private way through my hospice registered nurse case-managing experience. I served families in all ways, advocated for them before, during and after death. My role was expanded. I was an adjunct to hospice in my new role as an end-of life doula. I loved it. I served one family at a time. I loved every minute of it.

I began to blog, and people wrote to me. They wanted me to show them what I was doing. They wanted to train with me, and I sent them to hospice to learn, to serve there. In my mind, if you wanted to serve the dying, you'd go learn at hospice. These people kept coming back to me. I had more people writing and calling me to teach them than I had time available to serve them. It was an interesting time. I was meeting leaders in the movement before I realized we were in a movement. I simply wanted to do what I knew and loved in a more intimate way than I could within hospice. I knew from all my years of hospice case managing that people needed me and what I knew, long before they came to hospice. The point was driven home with the dying of my mother.

The straw that broke the camel's back happened for me in 2005 and sealed my commitment to educate people in a grassroots style. After my mother died and I came back to work at a long-term acute-care hospital, on my very first day, my patient was a woman with end-stage renal disease who was in her early sixties. I remembered her from before my mother's diagnosis and death just two months prior. She looked so sick, and she had been in there the whole time I was gone. As I came back from lunch, I walked in on our code team working on her in the middle of the hallway floor; it was drama, trauma, and violence on a woman who was dying.

They "saved" her life. She was a "do not resuscitate." That was my last shift at that hospital. I was far too tender after my mother's death at sixty-one to be in a position like that. I was far too staunch in my beliefs of proper care for the dying to watch it being done like this any longer. I had to help how I could, and I wanted to get out of "the trade," work for a living doing landscaping, and offer my "talent" as a death midwife as a community-based service for donation, one family at a time.

In the process of letting my community know I was around for this, to volunteer my time to help with supplying the best care possible during dying, I put an ad in a holistic directory. To do that, I thought I should call myself something descriptive so people would have an idea of what I was offering. I'd had my second child at home with lay midwives in an attempt to prevent another inappropriate C-section. I loved how all that unfolded, and in my mind, I was giving that same loving attention to people at a time that could otherwise be fraught with anxiety. Death midwife seemed like the fitting title. I put my ad in the holistic directory. The only response I received that whole year was from someone wanting me to train them.

One thing led to another, and thirteen years later, in 2018, I am here writing to you regarding my observations about this movement and the people I have been meeting who are called to it. No lack of passion in this bunch! Wow. Meeting people from all over the world, working in all sorts of professions, who are called to serve the dying too is amazing. Most of these people are not serving in a medical capacity. Interesting, isn't it?

There are so many people doing remarkable things all over this world, so many in our United States. They are people, just like me, who decided to do something positive for their communities, and they are pioneering as we speak. You will meet many remarkable people, so many names I wish I could list in this book for you look up as you would be a better person for meeting them. Most of them are not certified from an e doula program. I am not. I received my training and experience as a hospice RN with years in the field learning from a multidisciplinary team for many years. I stepped in to serve my community in a different capacity based on all those years of experience.

The phenomenon of a person taking an end-of-life doula training program is new. Most of us just went out and did the work to help others. But I can tell you over time, my phone rang incessantly, and person after person asked me to certify them. It didn't matter that I told them they didn't need certification. I could hear the passion in their voice, and I heard their stories. They were doing remarkable work already! I am told by other leaders of industries, such as the birth doula, yoga instructors, and aromatherapists, that this newest phase of having an end-of-life training program that certifies a person to become an end-of-life doula is an inevitable step in a movement such as ours.

These leaders have shared with me how their industries unfolded similarly. I can tell you from experience that this is led by the people themselves wanting to be doulas. It is not trainer-led. I had more people in my program demanding to be certified than not. We had debates and many discussions about this issue during my early years, and I have always followed what my clients wanted in service; it is no different in my training program. I decided in 2016 to join the end-of-life community in offering a CEOLD (certified end-of-life doula) Certificate from Quality of Life Care for people who successfully completed the requirements of my course. I fought this for ten years, but the day came when I realized I was serving no one by holding out on this.

Know there is much talent out here and so many people to learn from. We are all needed. As a practitioner, make sure you are responsible in what you know and what you offer the community. As a consumer, make sure you are comfortable with your practitioner and ask for referrals. Use your common sense. When you look into the eyes of the end-of-life doula before you, you will know if you are comfortable with them or not. Trust your gut.

II. **Palliative Care**

Almost every time I talk about palliative care, what I hear next is "What was that word?" "How do you say it?" Palliative is pronounced PAL-ee-uh-tiv; its Latin root means "to cloak." How in the world would you associate this word with anything medical? If a person does know the word, then the response is usually "Oh, yeah, hospice."

Know that palliative care should be offered and applied from day 1 of a serious diagnosis.

Hospice is just one way to apply palliative care; hospice is the application of palliative care as the sole method of care at the end of life.

As stated earlier, palliative care is also appropriate and successful in bringing and maintaining comfort for people as they deal with their serious illness, no matter where they are in the course of their disease. It is appropriate to begin palliative care as people begin cure-directed treatment for their serious illness, no matter what the illness is. It is appropriate no matter what treatment decisions people make, and it is appropriate long before hospice is even considered.

Let's get started with definitions. Notice how long each definition is. This is because of how involved it is. Also, it is a challenging concept to explain because its application in the non-hospice setting is relatively new. We who are in the trenches of palliative care are passionate about educating others on what it is in its fullness because the standard myth, among the public and healthcare workers alike, is still that it is "hospice." This is one of the biggest barriers to people's being comfortable as they deal with their serious illness.

The two definitions I am using are from the World Health Organization and the Center to Advance Palliative Care. Notice the similarities in the definitions. After reading these, you will know, whenever you see the definition of palliative care limited to "care that is implemented when cure is no longer possible," that the definition is inaccurate; that the definition is actually a definition of hospice care, not palliative care.

The World Health Organization's definition:
Palliative care is an approach that improves the quality of life of patients and their families facing the problems associated with life-threatening illness, through the prevention and relief of suffering by means of early identification and impeccable

assessment and treatment of pain and other problems, physical, psychosocial and spiritual.

Palliative care:

- ✓ provides relief from pain and other distressing symptoms;
- ✓ affirms life and regards dying as a normal process;
- ✓ intends neither to hasten or postpone death;
- ✓ integrates the psychological and spiritual aspects of patient care;
- ✓ offers a support system to help patients live as actively as possible until death;
- ✓ offers a support system to help the family cope during the patients' illness and in their own bereavement;
- ✓ uses a team approach to address the needs of patients and their families, including bereavement counseling, if indicated;
- ✓ will enhance quality of life, and may also positively influence the course of illness;
- ✓ is applicable early in the course of illness, in conjunction with other therapies that are intended to prolong life, such as chemotherapy or radiation therapy, and includes those investigations needed to better understand and manage distressing clinical complications.

The Center to Advance Palliative Care (CAPC) proposed definition of palliative care:

Until a US National Consensus can be reached, the CAPC Manual proposes that the following definition of palliative care be used to guide palliative care program development:

Brief Definition (8-second sound byte): Palliative Care aims to relieve suffering and improve the quality of living and dying.

Elaborated Definition: Palliative Care is appropriate for any patient and/or family living with, or at risk of developing a life-threatening illness

- ✓ due to any diagnosis
- ✓ with any prognosis regardless of age
- ✓ at any time they have unmet expectations and/or needs, and are prepared to accept care.
- ✓ It aims to address:
  - ✓ physical, psychological, social, spiritual and practical expectations and needs
  - ✓ loss, grief and bereavement

✓ preparation for, and management of, self-determined life closure, the dying process, and death

It is most effectively delivered by an interdisciplinary team. It may complement and enhance disease-modifying therapy, or it may become the total focus of care. . . . It may also be applicable to patients and families experiencing acute illness and/or chronic illness.

Now you know that you do not have to be dying to get palliative care. It is clear why it is so misunderstood. It is a relatively new concept, and new concepts require some time to take hold and become fully integrated in practice.

Palliative care begins when cure-directed treatment is begun with serious illness, and it ends with death. It is not to be started months after treatment. It is not to be used without expertly adjusting medications and dosages with meticulous assessments along the way. It is not to be taken away when someone is near death and appears to no longer be suffering just because he or she is unconscious and unresponsive.

Palliative care is to be utilized as any other form of treatment. It begins at diagnosis. It is monitored for effectiveness, and it is adjusted appropriately. Palliative medicine's effectiveness is based on the quality of life perceived by the person affected. Its success is measured by the comfortable functioning of the person.

With distressing symptoms that are not managed well, a person's life becomes very limited. Movement and participation in daily living are limited. When we are comfortable we are going to want to do some of our favorite things or just spend time with our thoughts. Appetite increases, energy increases, sleep improves, and this spiral of quality spins positively throughout the family, as we all deeply affect each other whether we get along or not.

To some of us, survival is the goal, no matter what the quality of life is. Our acute care medical system is set up for that, so you will receive lifesaving measures without having to ask for it. If you want anything different, you must make your wishes known in writing in the form of your advance directives.

What quality in living means to each of us is entirely personal. That is why we have to make our wishes known to our family and medical care team. There are no universal standards for quality of life, yet there is a universal assumption (within the hospital setting) that we all want to live as long as we possibly can, no matter the consequences.

As the awareness of the possibility of comfort throughout the course of a serious illness grows, so will the discussions of the full ramifications of our options in dealing with this illness. In these discussions, our power of choice will directly affect our own values regarding how we live with this kind of illness. The reality that we will be fully informed and make our decisions from that place will give us the dignity of having a say in our lives at this otherwise very powerless time.

We have little control over how our bodies react with illness, but we do have control over how we respond to it. Most of us don't know that we actually have this kind of power. There hasn't been the time to explain it. The medical staff have to experience it somehow to believe it. The side based on life at all costs is usually presented when a medical intervention is suggested. It takes a lot of time for those in the medical community to inform people of the quality-of-life issues that are a direct result of these interventions. Unfortunately, that kind of time is not built into our present system.

Yes, the piece that is missing is time, and a lack of time is the cause of much suffering prior to hospice entry. Many people never enter a hospice program and will die in hospitals. This happens because they have not been informed of the full ramifications of the treatments being offered because of either a lack of provider training or a lack of time. Many of these people live very uncomfortably during their last months or years.

The people who do enter a hospice program come in mostly during the last two weeks of life, and these admissions, as we would expect, are crisis-driven. They are usually crisis-driven admissions because people want to do everything possible to live a longer life. Many times, this focus leads to much suffering, as we all have seen. It is not necessary to choose between comfort and longevity of life. We can pursue longevity and have comfort as we do so. This is the good news. We do not have to forego quality of life to pursue a cure. We can have both. This is palliative care applied. We do not have to be dying to be comfortable. This is my message.

III. Hospice

Hospice services are for people who have been assessed and for whom it has been estimated that death will most likely occur within the next six months, if their disease continues on its present course.

Each country has its own system for referring you to this service and a different way of paying for it. Most developed countries do have hospice services. I work with many pioneers in other countries where hospice is virtually nonexistent. Those of us who actually do have a system to improve on are lucky indeed.

Hospice service is a multidisciplinary approach to caring for a person and his or her family holistically. Except for the volunteer, it is made up of a team of professionals:

- ✓ Physician
- ✓ Nurse
- ✓ Social worker
- ✓ Chaplain
- ✓ Certified nursing assistant
- ✓ Volunteer
- ✓ Bereavement counselor

There are many wonderful in-depth articles and books on hospice care and the history of hospice care. I know you will find them. In this chapter, I would like to emphasize three things about hospice services that you need to be aware of. Use this information to support people while they are on hospice.

1. Hospice works in a consultancy role; it is not designed to work as a caregiver agency.

    Many people are surprised to learn this. In hospice, we try to be there at key times, during rapid decline, and during the actual dying process if you want someone there. But the service itself is not designed to support a family for hours during the pre-death period. Hospice tries, when it is wanted in this way. That is why hospices will have "eleventh hour" volunteer programs and why some of them are developing end-of-life doula programs. Hospice goes to great lengths as a team to be present as much as possible during the deaths of people we care for, but as you can imagine, hospice is not staffed to support this.

2. Hospice utilizes palliative care as the sole method of care. No aggressive or cure-directed treatment options are offered within hospice. But there is so much that can be done at the end of life, so many treatment options, and they are all palliative (comfort) in nature. Much can be done to provide excellent medical and comfort care, and it is within the palliative medicine discipline to provide it.

3. People are not referred to hospice soon enough. There is a misunderstanding that hospice is only for the last few days of life. This cannot be further from the truth. The sooner people come to hospice with an end-stage illness, the better their symptoms will be managed, the more likely they will not have to go back to the hospital, and the more likely they are to eat more, sleep better, feel less pain, and feel better overall. They are more likely to live longer as well. All this is documented. A study is listed in "Resources" in this section about people living longer when they are on hospice services. It is because of the excellent care!

So, far from being depressing, hospice is an amazing benefit, with an eager team of professionals who want to help not only the person who is dying but also everyone else in the family. Realize that they are consultants; their role is to advise. They also provide great emotional, spiritual, and practical support. They provide durable medical equipment and pay for medications that relate to the terminal illness. They provide bathing and grooming care, plus light housekeeping in the vicinity of the dying person. They provide volunteers to assist the family when they can.

You can totally control how much of the team you want at your house, but you must see the nurse at least once every fourteen days to remain on service.

If you know someone who has been on the fence about choosing hospice, find out the biggest reason for their reluctance. They may simply be misinformed. Or their physician does not believe in hospice or does not recognize dying when he or she sees it or believes it is something to refer to when they are in their last week of life. Considering that hospice has been in the mainstream for fifty-six years, I find it amazing how late people are referred to hospice, even now. It doesn't have to be this way. As a guide, you can sensitively bring into awareness the benefits of an earlier admission to hospice.

IV. **End-of-Life Doula Training: Credentialing and Certification**

In the United States, there is no governing body, no regulating agency, no board that licenses or certifies any of us or the training we receive outside of the present medical system. We call ourselves what we want, for example, death doulas, end-of-life doulas, death midwives, end-of-life midwives, transition guides, end-of-life doulas, death coaches, amicus, soul midwife, soul guide, end-of-life practitioner, end-of-life specialist, and so many others!

We are self-regulating, so, give amazing service, 100 percent every time. I advise the people I work with to build and maintain relationships in their communities only with stellar individuals, like themselves, who have an impeccable practice doing whatever they are doing. Align yourself only with the best! Yes, we all will make mistakes, and top-of-the-line people will apologize and make it right. They will fix it to the best of their ability. Distance yourself from people who don't own their mistakes and who blame others for everything in their life.

When you look at various end-of-life programs, realize that each training program is created by the organization or by the person who created that organization. It is its, his, or her idea, and if the program has a certificate, it is an in-house certificate. No objective group of people have gotten together to decide that that program is the best or is measuring that program against some industry standard.

At this time, we are not organized under one umbrella board or association. Many people want this, and many other people don't. No association or organization that represents end-of-life doulas or doulas at this time is a joint effort of many trainers. The philosophy of those of us who don't want a credentialing board is we are not supportive of creating another layer of professionalism between people and their dying. We believe we are empowering people to care for their own dying and dead. We who are called to accompany are helping to bridge this time when people are seeking information about caring for their own families again.

Those who do want to be organized in this way are thinking about consumer safety for the most part, but there is also the issue of wanting the role legitimized and professionalized.

Enter the National End-of-Life Doula Alliance (NEDA). This organization is the only membership organization of end-of-life doulas that represents all training programs, not just one. NEDA is a brilliant move on the part of leading end-of-life doula trainers and sympathizers who wanted to join together to unify and empower the end-of-life doula professional role. I am proud to be a founding member and NEDA's first vice president since February 2018 to now. I stepped down at the close of the year to focus on my other leadership duties. It was an honor to help create standards of practice and core competencies for the end-of-life doula profession. There is much more work to do, but we have laid a fantastic foundation.

So right now, you may lean on NEDA for guidance about your practice, and if you decide you would like end-of-life doula training to ensure you will serve your community to the fullest, scout around and choose the training that feels right for you.

You decide what you want to learn and what feels good or appropriate to you at the time. You may want to learn about ceremony, ritual, and vigil; about creating and sustaining a practice; or about all of it! Decide which program speaks to your heart. You must research the program and decide if you want to learn from that teacher.

Consumer beware! Like everything else in your life, it is your responsibility to look into what you want and make sure it resonates with your values. Read "Consumer Guide to End-of-Life Training" in this section.

V. Consumer Guide to End-of-Life Training

I wrote this a couple of years ago and have seen nothing like it anywhere else since, so I am going to bring it to you here. This consumer guide is written for people who are new to end-of-life training, those who are not professionally involved in their present line of work.

There is a surge of worldwide interest by people looking for training to serve the dying either as part of their present practice or as a new way to serve people in their communities. Consequently, a great increase has also been observed in the number and kinds of trainings offered to meet the demand. You must consider many things when deciding which end-of-life training to take. Many wonderful programs exist. Be clear on exactly what you are looking for, and you will most likely find it.

For the most part, you will feel "right" about whomever you choose to work with, as that person or program will resonate with you at the time you are looking. I'd like you to be aware of a few things as you look over the vast array of trainings being offered all over the world.

The following information is my consumer's guide to end-of-life training, with a special focus on End-of-Life Doula "certification" issues.

Overall Considerations

In the end-of-life field, unless you work within hospice or special end-of-life positions within a hospital or a community organization (there are very few roles), it is hard to find a way to serve the dying "at the bedside" if you feel called to do this. Within hospice, paid positions include chaplain, nurse, social worker, and certified nursing assistant. There are volunteers, as well. That's it.

As the end-of-life field grows, other roles within the established healthcare systems and organizations will develop. I do have faith that end-of-life doulas will become more popular and will grow with the demand. It just will take time.

Special Focus: The End-of-Life Doula

A type of end-of life doula is gaining traction now, and it is called the *End-of-Life Doula*. This movement has been going on for many years and is gradually moving into the mainstream in the United States, the United Kingdom, and now Canada.

When I first started in 2005 in private practice, few programs were around. They were mostly through established schools and organizations, such as the Shira Ruskay Center in New York. The home-funeral industry was taking off then, and independent home-funeral-guide programs were being developed within that movement. I began to meet other people around the world, one by one, as we found each other, usually through blogging.

In 2010, I created my course, *"Accompanying the Dying: A Practical Guide and Awareness Training,"* in response to constant requests from people all over the world to share with them what I was doing and how I was doing it. It is amazing how many end-of-life doula programs there are now just a short eight years later. It is wonderful! There are some things to be mindful of though as you compare programs.

Not everyone who accompanies the dying and their families calls him- or herself a doula. There are many different names based on the concept of what a person will be doing. It is a highly individual preference for the person practicing. Some examples are death doula, doula for the dying, death midwife, midwife for souls, soul midwifery, transition guide, soul midwife, death coach, end-of-life doula, and many others.

But the word *doula* in relation to dying is definitely in the mainstream now as I write this, at the end of 2018. Many hospice programs, mostly in the northeastern United States and California and at a scattering of hospitals, are creating this support within their organizations. I am assisting them in the development of full end-of-life doula programs in multisite, multistate hospice systems, as well as the mom-and-pop operation.

Because it is finally in the mainstream, there are wonderful implications; but, just as in any other industry, there are also some things to watch for. One of those is the claim that you need a certain certification to practice as an end-of-life doula or guide. Know that is not true. At this time, there is no credentialing agency on any level.

Spotlight: Checklist for an End-of-Life Doula/Guide Program

I focus here directly on end-of-life doula programs (outside of home-funeral programs, as home-funeral programs are established and teach a specific skill set). At this time, September 2018, you see more training programs for end-of-life doulas than for end-of-life guides, midwives, or specialists, but they are in the same family of training: serving others at the end of life. Because end-of-life doulas can be focused on many different services, I want you to be very clear about what you are seeking in training so that you will be getting exactly what you want.

Also keep in mind that sometimes people who have never served in this way have written me about end-of-life doula programs they were setting up. Sometimes their program sounded lovely, but how can a person train you to do something and know about the specific issues involved when he or she has never done it personally?

To train you to operate within an organized system within a hospice, a hospital, or a community group is one thing; to train you as a personal End-of-Life Doula in independent practice is quite another. There are great programs for all of it. But which do you want? I would like you, as a consumer, to consider the following when you are looking specifically for an end-of-life doula program.

The Program Itself

1. Is it a program that will train you to volunteer with an organization's program? Or is it one that will train you to do individual work?
2. Is the program training you for a special skill or in a general way?
3. Is the program stating you must complete its program to be certified to practice as an end-of-life doula? As so many ways exist to serve the dying at the end of life, most experienced doulas and midwives to the dying who have worked in the movement over many years agree: *We don't want a regulating agency determining who is qualified.* The whole point of what most of us are doing is a desire to bring care for the dying and death care back into the community and to share the wisdom with each other, not create yet another professional role.

   Since 2005, I have been in this movement talking with others all over the world who have trailblazed this path, and *very* few people in the industry whom I know are in favor of a credentialing or certifying agency's telling us what can or cannot or should or should not be done. We are too individualistic. Sometimes our only unifying bond is the people we serve.

   We all want consumers to be safe and trainers to be skilled and knowledgeable. We are facing the same issues that yoga instructors, birth doulas, aromatherapists, and other practitioners have faced in their beginnings.
4. The "certificate" that you receive from each program—any program—is an in-house certificate only; it means that you completed that particular program. It takes years to develop a good reputation demonstrating that your program is sound. Both old and new programs exist all over the world. The better ones never state that you have to have their program to be recognized or to practice.

The Instructor(s)

1. Is the person training you to become a private end-of-life doula? Or are you being trained to be an end-of-life doula within an organization or community group?
2. If he or she is training you to become a private end-of-life doula, is the person an end-of-life doula him- or herself? Has he or she ever been? For how many years has he or she served?
3. How long has the teacher been experienced in caring for families independently, not as part of an agency or organization?
4. Is the program creator drawing from education, training, and personal experiences? It is fine to create a program based on a theory that you have become passionate about. This is done all the time; just know from whom you are learning.
5. What is the background of the person teaching the course? Are those the skills you want to learn?
6. Is the person an experienced educator?

Comparing End-of-Life Training Programs (All Kinds)

Most programs teach an overall view of end-of-life concepts and things to be mindful of when you serve the dying. Some programs focus on a certain skill or window of time during the process for example, vigils, death care, after-death care, home funerals, and so on. Your first question should be, "Am I looking for an overview or for a specific skill or concept?"

These programs are usually taught by someone or a group of people who have invaluable end-of-life training in some capacity, like a physician, a nurse, a chaplain, a social worker, a death educator, or an end-of-life doula or midwife. They can give you priceless insights about how to serve the dying from their own perspective on how they do it.

They should know the issues involved, be subject-matter experts, and have the passion and the calling to serve. Check out the program's background and find out where its instructors acquired most of their experience. If they are training you, that is what you are going to learn: what they know within their system of reference.

Following are the various training options for learning the material, along with a description of what makes them unique.

Correspondence/Online/Teleseminar Courses

These types of courses vary between self-paced and group instructor-led trainings. The amount of feedback you receive depends on your instructor, so check out instructor involvement carefully. Most of these are self-paced, and there is no interaction with the instructor. You can download videos or education materials and work through them at your leisure.

Seminar Course

Seminar courses typically span a day or two or up to a week in a group setting. Usually this will be in lecture style and offer small-group breakout exploratory sessions.

School-Based

These are usually at a university level or at a school known specifically for death education. The classes are more formal and structured and usually involve a committed time period or are weekend-intensive, as well as material learned in a classroom setting or online.

One-to-One Mentoring

You are working with the instructor personally, developing your understanding and integration of the material and of how you want to use it, as you learn.

Mixture of Correspondence and Group Training

Some programs require an intense commitment of time and participation and include a lengthy experiential group component. Make sure you are willing to carve out the time you will need.

Tips and Warnings

1. All programs are not created equal. Decide what is most important to you. Are you just looking for information? Do you want a specific new skill? Do you want more of

a certain philosophy? Do you want to build a practice? Do you want to supplement what you are learning within the volunteer program in which you are participating?

2. From whom do you want to learn: A physician? A spiritual or religious person? An end-of-life doula? A registered nurse? A death educator? Someone who runs a school?

3. What is your style of learning? Do you want to read and write essays? Do you want to self-explore? Do you want just the facts? Do you want to be mentored over time? Do you want hands-on learning? Do you want to be with a group?

4. Watch out for any program that suggests you need to have their program to practice as an end-of-life "whatever." When you purchase that trainer's program, you are not recognized by any one licensing or credentialing board. An End-of-Life Doula credential is not necessary to practice.

Which Program Should I Choose?

When people contact me for training, I ask them to do the following:

Put some time aside, at least an hour. Center yourself spiritually. Write out on paper with pen in your handwriting how you want to serve the dying. If you had all the money and time and energy in the world, how would you want to do it? There is your vision; now find your training to make that happen.

Write about some of the following also:

1. Do I just want information for information's sake?
2. Do I want a self-paced system with no interaction with an instructor?
3. Do I want to be part of a group?
4. Do I want to hear from a particular voice? A religious view, spiritual teaching, professional angle, university setting?
5. Do I have a goal of a private practice in mind?
6. Do I want one-to-one mentoring?
7. Do I enjoy group intensives over one or two days?
8. Do I want hands-on learning? Face-to-face learning?
9. Are Skype/phone calls enough for me? Do I need face-to-face time?
10. Would I enjoy small group mentoring?

Other Tips

Once you have answered the preceding questions, it will be easier to compare programs as you will be focused on exactly how you want to learn the information.

As you peruse all the websites, note the ones you are drawn to. Yes, it's marketing, but the person who created that had a say or built the whole thing personally. Although it isn't the packaging you are putting heavy thought into (the person may not be good at that), you are getting a sense of the person's energy and what is important for him or her to relay.

How does your heart feel when you talk to the teacher? Great? Skeptical? Tenuous? Safe? Do you want to explore further? Or do you have a nagging feeling this isn't right for you? Listen to your inner voice!

Talk to at least three of the instructors or narrow it down to three courses. Sleep on it. You usually have a sense of what to do after this.

Finally, if you had all the money in the world and could take any of the three, which would you choose? Do that one. Usually, we find the money to do exactly what we want. Here is no exception.

Make the process enjoyable! You are investing a lot of time and energy into pursuing your dream. It should be honored and a joy to do so. Good luck!

VI. **Leading Your Community**

You do not have to be a doula in private practice to be a leader in your community and facilitate more awareness. To be an advocate for death empowerment, you need to create spaces for gatherings and venues for sharing safely. Death Café is such a platform. You can download a kit to host a death café, if there is none in your area, and begin the conversation!

You may want to start your own book club or movie club or art projects. There are so many ways to gather those who are interested in empowering themselves in the planning of their own death and bringing awareness and choice to their own loved ones.

Think about what you love to do, your own schedule, and your own needs, and see where there is time in your schedule naturally. Create a two-hour session of some kind that will enable people to explore their own hearts. Then enjoy the process! Share what you are doing with others around your city, state, and country.

Network and collaborate with other death leaders in your community. Find out what is being done and where you may be helpful with what is already established. Many hands make for lighter work. We have a lot to do, but we don't have to do it alone or reinvent the wheel. Plug in! There is no such thing as competition in this. Collaboration is where it is at!!

An example of this is what two other end-of-life doula trainers and I did. Patty Burgess-Brecht asked several trainers to come together for an event. Those who said yes were Suzanne O'Brien and I. After some discussion, we decided what was needed most at this time was a focus on doulas in healthcare. We all had extensive experience in healthcare and hospice from a variety of angles and had so much to contribute together. At the end of 2017, Professional Doula International was created and our inaugural launch of the training was in New York City in September 2018.

This specialty training for end-of-life doulas is not a foundational training. A doula must have that already. We created this comprehensive add-on training for end-of-life doulas and other professionals who want to advocate for people in healthcare as we believe that end-of-life doulas are the answer to the oncoming crisis we are facing in the next twenty-five years.

Our training is called the National Professional End-of-Life Doula Certification (NPEC). We believe that NPEC will be the training that end-of-life doulas and healthcare entities value and trust to know that they will have optimum knowledge to work alongside healthcare teams and understand the dynamics and the goals of each system.

VII. **Advance Directives**

Have yours done first. Before you go out and teach others about this, make sure yours are done and at least two people know where they are. In Texas you should have the following six forms completed:

1. *Medical Power of Attorney.* This form appoints who will speak for you in the event you cannot speak for yourself while you are alive.
2. *Directives to Physicians.* This form tells physicians, your healthcare team, and your family what medical treatments you want under certain conditions. You can state what you want as well as what you don't want.
3. *Durable Power of Attorney.* This form appoints who will speak for you to handle your financial and legal affairs should you be unable to do so for yourself while you are still alive.
4. *Body Disposition Authorization.* Fill out this form to ensure you will be cremated.
5. *Appointment of Agent to Control Disposition of Remains.* This form appoints the person who will make sure your wishes are complied with regarding your body after death.
6. *Out-of-Hospital Do Not Resuscitate.* This is a form to have that will ensure you will not receive CPR outside of the hospital setting. If you are found dead outside of the hospital setting and someone calls 911 out of panic, you must have this form to show. Otherwise, emergency personnel are required to perform CPR.

Find out which forms are necessary to handle your affairs in your area of the world. In the United States, to see what specific forms you need for your state, check in with Caring Connections (a program of the National Hospice and Palliative Care Organization), the Funeral Consumer Alliance, and the Conversation Project, for starters. The forms listed earlier should work for every US state, but make sure you have them for where you live in the world.

Have your will in place and an executor to handle your affairs after you die. The Durable Power of Attorney indicates how your affairs should be handled if you are unable to do so while you are still alive, and your executor handles them after your death. You need to appoint a person for each role. You can have the same person for each role.

VIII. **End-of-Life Task List**

Earlier in the book, I referred to an end-of-life task list that I created. Volumes have been written so eloquently about what is happening on every level with us as we die. What I created here is simply a checklist so that you can create your own systems of dealing with it and helping a person to check off their tasks. Don't be afraid to ask; most people are doing it in their head, believe me. They may not call it an end-of-life task list, but it is on most dying people's minds if they are conscious and aware.

This list is in no particular order:

1. Who is going to take care of them, and where will they die?
2. Who is going to take care of their animals?
3. Who is going to get their most important personal possessions?
4. They want to process how they feel without taking care of others' feelings.
5. They want you to quit trying to make them feel better about it and instead just listen, without trying to fix it.
6. They want to grieve their losses.
7. They are worried about the most important people in their life, and they want to know they will be okay.
8. They want to be forgiven.
9. They want to forgive.
10. They want to be known.
11. They want to do some final trips, visits, events, bucket-list items, and so on.
12. They want people to know how they really feel—sometimes for the first time.

And some other important things on their mind:

➤ They want to be left alone sometimes.
➤ Sometimes they want to die before they do, and they are angry that they are not dying fast enough.
➤ They want to have made a difference.
➤ Sometimes they don't want to refer to their dying at all. It is all they can do to cope with it, without words solidifying it. It may be too much for them to

discuss. Don't assume that they are not having closure or that their death is not a "good death."

We do not know what is in a person's heart. What we can do to help with the "good death" is not to add drama but, instead, to love ourselves, the person dying, and the people in our circle. When in doubt, take the high road. You can always apologize later for not reacting and for not making a fool of yourself in trying to force solutions and outcomes.

IX. **Pre-Death Vigil and Post-Death Vigil Plan Checklists**

I created these two vigil plans, the "Pre-Death Vigil Plan" and the "Death and Post-Death Vigil Plan," one year for one of my students for her education sessions.

It is a suggested format for gathering the information necessary to create the dying experience you wish to have. Not only will the loving details you provide here for your loved ones to carry out give you the experience you want but those details will also help them in their grieving, knowing they have done all in their power to carry out and honor your wishes.

You may use these forms for your personal use. If you want to use them for professional use, please write us and ask for our branded handout and we will send that to you. Write us at danielle.cochran@qualityoflifecare.com

Please answer the following with the period of your last days in mind, the days immediately preceding your death.

Pre-Death Vigil Plan

The room where you will be lying:
1. What room do you want to be in?
2. How do you want the lighting? Do you want the shades drawn? The windows open? What is your preference, weather permitting?
3. Do you want anyone to be able to come in who wants to see you, share time with you, and love you?
4. Are you clear that you only want specific people with you? Who are they?
5. Under what circumstances would it be okay for someone to be in this room who is not on your known list?
6. Is there anyone that you do not want present at any time?
7. Do you want one or two people at a time, or is it okay if there is a group?
8. Do you want this room quiet?
9. Do you want people to be able to talk and share stories with you in this room? Or do you want it to be a contemplative space only?
10. Do you want music playing close to you? What kind? Do you want it day and night, only during the day, or only at night?
11. Do you have a list of songs you would like to hear, as you are dying these last days?

12. Do you want aromatherapy ongoing in a diffuser? Do you want it delivered by some other means?
13. Do you want strong odors away from you? What would be the exception?
14. Do you want candles?
15. Do you care if the candles are real or fake (battery-operated), scented or unscented? Please state your preference.
16. Do you want to be in your pajamas, or do you want a "street" blouse or T-shirt showing? What do you want visible on your upper body as people are going in and out of your room?
17. As you are dying and unconscious, what do you want happening? Give some instructions. What do you not want happening?

In the rest of the house:
1. Do you want the rest of the house in a contemplative state, or is it okay if there is laughter and such?
2. Do you want the TV going on? Music? Do you want to leave it up to whoever is there?

Regarding your caregiver(s):
1. Whom do you want caring for you in the last days?
2. Do you want someone there around the clock or just checking on you in normal intervals?
3. Do you want hospice services to support you and your loved ones?
4. How would you want your caregiver to be supported as they care for you? What would be important to you for your caregiver to have available?
5. What words do you want them to know if you could tell them during these days? What words can you offer them to hold on to as they care for you? What do you want for them?

The final hour:
1. If it is foreseen that you are in your final breaths, is it okay that everyone who is present is there? Do you only want certain people?
2. What support do you want as you are taking your last breaths?
3. Once you are dead, is there anything you want done to you or for you in the moments or first hour after your death?
4. Do you want a small gathering or a big funeral?

Additional thoughts:

Please write any additional thoughts below that would be helpful to your loved ones.

Death and Post-Death Vigil Plan

In the period of imminent death and in the hours and days afterward, what would you prefer to happen? Create your plan.

Imminent death:
1. Who do you want at your bedside as you are imminently dying?
2. Do you have a preference for how your bedside environment is, as you are imminently dying? Or do you want whatever may be comfortable for your significant others who are caring for you?
3. What is your preference for your bedside environment; what do you want? Do you want candlelight? Music?
4. At your bedside, do you want everyone who wants to be there present? Do you want only two or three people at a time?
5. Do you want people to pray or meditate for you during this time? Aloud? Silently?
6. Do you want prayers or words of hope read to you? What do you want read to you aloud, if anything?
7. Do you want people singing?

Death:
1. In the moments following your death, do you want any spiritual or religious practices done?
2. Do you want anything read?
3. Do you want your body cleansed? Anointed? Certain clothing put on?
4. Do you want any certain ritual performed?
5. Is it okay if the area around your body receives tokens, flowers, or mementos by others?
6. Do you want to be left alone? For how long?

In the hours and days following death:
1. Do you want a public vigil for a certain length of time?

2. How long do you want your body kept at home? (If you are not home, the facility will have limits.)
3. Whom do you want to transport your body to the crematory or cemetery or funeral home?
4. Do you want to be buried in a traditional cemetery? Or do you want to be buried in an environmentally friendly cemetery known as a "green cemetery"? A green cemetery ensures that all processes and products used in burial are friendly to the environment and will not harm it.
5. Do you want a ceremony to celebrate your life? Who do you want to be the celebrant/officiant?
6. What do you want to happen at your ceremony?
7. Would you like to record your thoughts in writing or video for the people at your ceremony or to be available to certain loved ones?
8. Have you prepared an ethical will or some type of legacy document that expresses your values and what you hope for the people you love that can be shared at your service?
9. Have you considered a home funeral? If so, arrangements must be made to keep the body cool.

X. **Accidents, Violent Deaths and Suicide**

In my end-of-life mentoring community, many people come through our program who want to offer support to people dying from accidents, violent death, and suicide. If the person does not die instantly, usually hospice is not called for these deaths, and sometimes the need for support is more than the hospital chaplains and volunteer support staff at the hospital can handle.

If you are interested in providing vigil support to people dying from tragic circumstances, get in touch with Victims Services within the Police Department in your town. Also make an appointment with the hospital chaplain and find out what kind of support they need and what kind of training you must do to help. These are great places to begin. Ask what process you need to go through to be available to people and their families at this time.

If you are interested in supporting the loved ones left behind, make sure you get the best awareness and skills training to accompany people through these events. You will be focusing on accompanying people through grief as a companion unless you are a trained and experienced therapist, chaplain, social worker, or other health professional or healer.

There is a place for the professional therapist and social worker, of course, and there is also a place for a friend in grief, a companion to the person who is reeling from the shocking death of a loved one. In our program we refer to this role as bereavement companion. Do not underestimate the value of this role just because it is not a licensed role. Your role as a bereavement companion is to listen and accompany and love the person as they stabilize themselves.

XI. **The Sacred, Ceremony, Ritual**

Every day, what I hear most from people who call me is their desire to accompany a person and his or her family as those individuals wish, surrounded by love and beauty and meaningful interactions and practices.

They want to engage with a person and his or her family as that person and the family wish, without an agenda of their own.

They also want to help keep the sacred energy and space of this great transition for the family and nourish it. Sometimes people want us to create ceremony or rituals for them because they are really at a loss for how to create a ceremony on their own. They may overlook their own rituals as powerful and meaningful. Ceremony for some can be elaborate or as simple as compassionate presence, loving energy, silence, and maybe some aromas or items from nature brought into the room.

What is sacred to one family is unique, and our role with them is to be curious about what is meaningful to them. It is not for us to whip out our own special ideas and assume they will want those. It is wonderful to have our own books of poems and songs and our bags with candles, oils, cloth, and more. We just need to remember that we are their servants, and there is nothing more personal than ritual and ceremony as someone you love is dying.

Many beautiful books and articles have been written about creating ceremony. I offer some very simple but powerful tips to get you started, in case you are unfamiliar with this yourself or not yet comfortable:

1. Remember that you are weaving a practice together with the family. You will not be creating something out of thin air but are asking them what is important to them and to the dying person. You will have a conversation, and ideas will flow. One thing will lead to another. Have faith in this.

2. The tools of ceremony are simple: candles, cloth, prayers, songs, oils, sage, leaves, sticks, flowers, incense, art supplies, singing, dancing, and music. Take your pick! When you let go of "performing" and get into the energy of the family you are with, you will be able to hear what they are saying and want.

3. Make suggestions and go with their "yes." It is good enough. The creation is from everyone's input and presence. Remember, this is not about you. You are merely a facilitator.

4. Have a basic formula that you get used to. For example, begin with a moment of silence, then by an invocation or prayer, then by someone from the family offering words or a prayer, and then maybe with everyone saying something specific that you have asked or bringing an object to an alter or something similar, followed by music and a closing prayer. You can have a simple structure through which you weave countless beautiful alternatives. You may need your structure only a few times and will feel comfortable to let it go.

5. For a more formal ceremony, it would be best to be trained in performing ceremonies. Don't go beyond your skill level when a family asks you to serve them in this way. Tell them the truth of your level of expertise and see if they are willing to explore with you.

6. Know that the more ritual and ceremony you bring in with the family, the more healing it can bring and help facilitate their grieving.

XII. **Bereavement Support**

This entire book is a guide, not only in assisting others at the end of life but also in assisting them in their bereavement. We know that planning for our dying, feeling empowered in our choices, and creating the experience we want will aid us in our grieving and in our bereavement.

Planning ahead is a part of bereavement support. Helping our loved ones have the dying experience they want and being a part of this whole process weaves the experience in strength, love, and choice. This helps us move forward after our loved ones die.

Many people will never seek "bereavement services." They will cope on their own or with the support of family and friends.

For the people who do want extra support, there are many online bereavement support groups, and many hospices have excellent bereavement services as well.

A new platform called the "Dinner Party" is a bereavement support for young people. Instead of going to a group and talking, they have a series of dinner parties or potlucks and talk about their experiences more naturally than in a formal group in a center or therapist's office.

Many people I work with in my programs are incorporating bereavement visits in their practice. They are creating a very natural service that has continuity from pre-death through various times after death.

Integrating a loved one's death and our new life without them takes time. We need to actively make the choice to do so. It is not abnormal to miss someone we love for years after their death. We are never the same after someone we love dies; we are forever changed. Love does that to us.

Learn what you can about grief from people who are not afraid to call it what it is. Read from the likes of Stephen Jenkinson and Terri Daniel. Visit Zenith Virago's website and see what she is up to in Australia in honoring grief and celebrating life. Read about home funerals and how they help in the grieving process. I'm mentioning just a few resources here that you may not have heard of and that will definitely prod your present consciousness.

XIII. **Resources**

Every resource I mentioned in this book is listed here in alphabetical order. I know the URLs for these websites change over time, so I am just listing the name of the organization, report or the initiative only. Please type the name into your chosen search engine (e.g., Google, Yahoo, or Bing), should you desire to investigate them further.

Careflash

Caring Connections

Center to Advance Palliative Care

"Comparing Hospice and Nonhospice Patient Survival Among Patients Who Die Within a Three-Year Window" in the *Journal of Pain and Symptom Management*

Compassion and Choices

Death Café

Death Over Dinner

Die Wise, by Stephen Jenkinson

Doorway Into Light

Death Café

Dinner Party

End-of-Life Doula Advisory Council (within the NHPCO)

End-of-life Practitioners Collective

Funeral Consumer Alliance

Get Palliative Care

Journey with Deanna (blog and podcast)

National End-of-Life Doula Alliance

National Home Funeral Alliance

National Hospice and Palliative Care Organization

National Professional End of Life Doula Certification (NPEC)

Professional Doula International

School of Accompanying the Dying

Quality of Life Care

Terri Daniel

The Conversation Project

World Health Organization

Zenith Virago

Acknowledgments

I would like to acknowledge every single person I ever assisted through dying and every person whom I have served through this process. You taught me everything I know, and I am honored to have served you.

My children, Danielle and Lauren, give me more joy than I can say. Danielle has made my work possible in this movement on every level, and we all owe her everything she could ever wish for in this life! Thank you. The support of my brother and sister and their families has meant everything to me along this journey, and my father's advice to "Do what you love" fills me when I get down. I am one lucky woman to have so many loyal and rich friendships and so many people in my circle who are strong and caring and follow their own hearts. And I treasure the love and support of my partner, Mary Hilburn, for bringing me to the country and for all the laughter! And I thank my friend Cathy Chapaty for giving this book a once-over during the first edit. Your feedback was invaluable! And my deepest gratitude goes to Melissa Tullos for gifting me with her expertise in editing this manuscript for me in a special way. I asked her for a very specific eye and she accomplished the task brilliantly. And thank you Stan Wilson, my dear friend, for reviewing this book for me. Your friendship and support over the years in my work means the world to me; you have been with me since the beginning.

Mary Burgess, thank you for being my key grounding force through the shocking and rapid dying of my mother. The fact that you were my first mentor when I was a brand-new hospice nurse in 2000 makes it even more special. My mother's dying and death is the root of my work today, and you held me up during this time; you were my doula.

I honor my healers and teachers on this journey. My own commitment to self-care and the healing of mind/body/spirit has brought to me the most amazing people, sharing their wisdom and powerful gifts with me over the years. Thank you from the bottom of my heart. It's surprising to me how in our earnestness to be all we can be to others, that we neglect our own selves in the process—and not even realize it. My eyes have been opened to this in my own life and I thank Dr. Martin and my alternative health care team for their compassionate care and not giving up on me.

I honor the people over my lifetime, those that are new to me and old, and those who have disappeared from my life for a variety of reasons. My heart will never forget you. You and I shared love, and I am better because I knew and loved you.

I thank and honor my many death-worker colleagues over the years as we have batted ideas around and walked with each other as we figured out our way. There are too many to name here, and for that I am extremely grateful.

I want to acknowledge the Great Spirit, God, The Divine Feminine, One-Who-Cannot-Be-Named, The-Unnamable-One, The-One-who-has-a-1,000-names and yet is still so hard for us to define. I am blessed because I know I am strengthened not by my best thinking but because I lean on my Spiritual Source.

I thank God for the spiritual world and that it is my perfect food. I am fed so richly by it and by the gifts of this earth, the stars, and the infinite universe. I am grateful for the love of the Father, the Mother, the Grandmothers, and the Grandfathers. I am grateful for Jesus, my most holy influence. I am thankful that I am not limited by my or your limiting beliefs. I am so thankful that I am finally out of my cage. You will find me listening to the whispers in the wind, placing my belly on the earth, hearing with my heart, crying my heart out to God, taking in the manna from the heavens. I'm so grateful my spiritual path has brought me to where I am now. Every single step it has taken me to get here has been worth it.

I am deeply grateful to each of my colleagues who endorsed this book. It was from my deep respect for your work that I made the request, and it means the world to me that I knew you well enough to ask.

To Sharon Lund, I had no idea that day as we lounged on the beach in Maui that you were a publisher. I just knew I'd found a new friend. Thank you for publishing my book with Sacred Life Publishers. To Lynette Smith, you edited my words and turned them into harmony. Wendy Jo Dymond, for the second edit as well as final edit. To Miko Radcliffe, graphic design artist, you took my vision of my cover and made it a masterpiece. Danielle's beautiful photography of our cover and of my picture is the beautiful cherry on the cake!

And to you, Reverend Bodhi Be, I came to you to learn and in the process found a brother and friend. Your love means the world to me.

About the Author

Deanna Cochran, RN

Deanna Cochran is an RN, End-of-Life Educator, Doula Mentor and Program Developer. She is one of the earliest voices within the end-of-life doula movement and has been serving people with serious illness and the people who serve them since 2000.

After the death of her mother, she began to serve others as a death midwife and began educating about pre-hospice palliative care. She created Quality of Life Care, LLC (QLC) in 2005 and year after year has responded to the requests of the people who came to her: training end of life doulas, providing end-of-life doula program development to hospices, creating public education initiatives for consumers and fellow end-of-life practitioners, and mentoring pioneers around the world as they create innovative services for their communities.

Deanna has trained thousands of people over the years with her innovative approach that put end-of-life doula training on the map in 2010—the only program of its kind worldwide. The School of Accompanying the Dying is a powerful method providing deep transformation and confidence for the doula within a world class end-of-life doula curriculum, "Accompanying the Dying: A Practical Guide and Awareness Training."

She is thrilled to be a founding member and first Vice President of the National End of Life Doula Alliance and is honored to serve as Chair of the NHPCO End-of-Life Doula Advisory Council. She is a grateful member of the training team for the first 3 years of Doorway into Light's annual International Death Doula Conference, which utilizes her curriculum in their yearly certification.

She has always valued unity in the movement and collaborates regularly for special projects she sees as highly needed to bring solutions to our dying. She is Partner in Professional Doula International with Doing Death Differently and Doulagivers International, leading the way for end-of-life doulas to be advocates within mainstream healthcare. She also is Partner with Suzanne O'Brien with The National Certificate for End of Life Doula Hospice Programs (NCEHP), a powerful end of life doula program template for hospices, complete with not only step by step instructions but also proven trainings and systems for full integration within the hospice team

Deanna's innovative leadership style has gained the attention of corporate healthcare providers as well as small businesses and community educators. QLC's Education Partner program provides a proven system and solid foundation for their end-of-life training needs. Many use her core curriculum in their branded programs.

QLC offers free public education through a variety of platforms. QLC's free Community Discussion Program will be launched in 2019, providing 10 lessons for independent educators throughout the country to facilitate discussions with people in their own communities. She has also developed a specific role for the doula serving in the serious illness time period (before hospice), called Supportive CareDoula®. Stay tuned for more information on this very specific role.

Deanna has created many public service initiatives, which have been used and copied all over the world. She created the world's first podcast show devoted to palliative care from diagnosis through bereavement, *The Journey Radio,* in 2014. It has since been transformed to *Journey with Deanna,* a blog and podcast continuing to educate and inform about palliative and end of life issues. She interviews leading international experts, the average non–medically oriented person living and dying in this world, as well as sharing personal stories and thoughts on trending topics in the field.

She created The End-of-life Practitioner's Collective (ELPC) in 2014, which has been her labor of love joining families with end-of-life practitioners in private practice who work alongside of their present healthcare teams. The ELPC directory is for consumers to find independent end-of-life practitioners for a variety of services in one place. There is no other centralized place where people can find this kind of holistic support focusing on the end-of-life period. Join us in the collective at www.endoflifepro.org if you are a practitioner. You may join as a professional, community volunteer, or community resource.

Since 2000, Deanna has dedicated her life to empowering people to live and die exactly as they wish—with as much comfort, peace, and choice as possible. Visit our Free Learning Center on Facebook, https://www.facebook.com/journeywithDeanna.

She has been proudly featured in *The New York Times*, *Medscape*, *Quartz*, *Pacific Standard*, *The Austin American Statesman*, *Story Corps*, and many other publications, podcasts, and radio programs.

If this book has inspired you to explore more deeply, please join us in our school of Accompanying the Dying. Learn more at www.school.accompanyingthedying.com.

Blessings on your journey.

CPSIA information can be obtained
at www.ICGtesting.com
Printed in the USA
LVHW050714131120
671375LV00009B/285

9 780989 659352